Credit and Debit Cards: Federal Use

CREDIT AND DEBIT CARDS: FEDERAL USE

UNITED STATES GOVERNMENT ACCOUNTABILITY OFFICE

Nova Science Publishers, Inc.
New York

For permission to use material from this book please contact us:
Telephone 631-231-7269; Fax 631-231-8175
Web Site: http://www.novapublishers.com

LIBRARY OF CONGRESS CATALOGING-IN-PUBLICATION DATA

Available Upon Request
ISBN 978-1-60692-351-1

Published by Nova Science Publishers, Inc. ✣ New York

CONTENTS

Abbreviations

CFO	Chief Financial Officer
DeCA	Defense Commissary Agency
DOJ	Department of Justice
FMS	Financial Management Service
FTC	Federal Trade Commission
GDP	gross domestic product
GSA	General Services Administration
IAA	Israel Antitrust Authority
IRS	Internal Revenue Service
NAFI	nonappropriated fund instrumentality
OMB	Office of Management and Budget
PIN	personal identification number
RBA	Reserve Bank of Australia
TILA	Truth in Lending Act
VA	Department of Veterans Affairs

CORRESPONDENCE

May 15, 2008

Congressional Requesters:

Consumers increasingly use credit and debit cards to make payments, including those to federal, state, and local governments for such things as park admission fees, driver licenses, and income taxes. According to a federal banking regulator, 47 billion credit and debit card transactions occurred in 2006, exceeding the approximately 31 billion check payments made that year.[1] As with other forms of payment, merchants and government entities incur various costs to accept credit or debit cards. The majority of the costs associated with accepting cards are the "merchant discount fees" paid to the banks that merchants use to process their transactions. Generally, for each Visa or MasterCard transaction, a portion of the merchant discount fee is paid from the merchant's bank—called the acquiring bank—to the bank that issued the card. This portion, called the interchange fee, reimburses card issuers for a portion of the costs they incur in providing card services.[2] The balance of the merchant discount fee is retained by the acquiring bank to cover its costs of providing services. In addition to these fees, government entities that accept cards also incur other, less significant costs to install and maintain necessary equipment and to transmit card transaction data.

Interchange fee amounts are calculated using rates, typically between 1 and 2 percent of a purchase's value.[3] The two largest card networks (Visa and MasterCard) establish default interchange rates for their respective

---

[1]Federal Reserve System, *The 2007 Federal Reserve Payments Study: Noncash Payment Trends in the United States: 2003-2006* (Dec. 10, 2007).

[2]In most cases the acquiring bank and the issuing bank for Visa and MasterCard transactions are different institutions. In contrast, American Express and Discover are "proprietary" networks that act as both the issuing and acquiring entities. As a result, they retain the entire amount of the merchant discount fee they receive from merchants' sales to American Express and Discover card users. Accordingly, American Express and Discover transaction fees are included in the total merchant discount fee amounts presented in this report, but not in the interchange fee amounts.

[3]Interchange rates are typically a percentage of the payment amount plus a fixed fee per transaction (for example, $0.05 or $0.10). In some cases, the interchange rate may be a flat rate per transaction (for example, $0.75).

systems.[4] According to officials from one card network, in establishing default interchange rates, the networks take into consideration competitive factors of both card issuers and merchants as well as certain costs that are associated with issuing and accepting cards. Interchange rates vary according to a number of factors, including the type of merchant accepting the card, the method used to transmit the transaction information, and the type of card used. For example, "reward" credit cards, which provide their holders with cash rebates or points, typically have a higher interchange rate than standard credit cards. That is, a merchant accepting a reward credit card, depending on the merchant's agreement with its acquiring bank, may pay a higher merchant discount fee for a purchase made with a reward credit card. Additionally, if a cardholder uses a debit card and enters a personal identification number (PIN), rather than signing a receipt to authorize the transaction, the transaction generally poses less risk to the card issuer, partly because the identity of the cardholder is more certain and therefore the interchange rate is lower.

As the popularity of credit and debit cards for making purchases and payments has grown, so has the amount of merchant discount fees paid by the merchants—including federal government entities—that accept cards. One source estimates more than $36 billion in interchange fees was paid in 2006.[5] These fees have been the subject of litigation in the United States, but they are not federally regulated. In some other countries, government authorities have taken steps to limit the amounts of these fees.

In addition to accepting cards for payments, federal entities also use cards to make purchases. The General Services Administration (GSA) administers the SmartPay® program, which provides cards for federal entities to purchase goods and services, including office supplies, fuel for government vehicles, and airline tickets and hotel visits for employees on

[4]Both Visa and MasterCard developed as membership organizations consisting of banks that participated in their respective payment systems. Because of this structure, traditionally they were referred to as credit card associations. MasterCard restructured to become a publicly held corporation, making its initial public offering of certain classes of stock in March 2006. Similarly, Visa became public, initiating its initial public offering during March 2008. For purposes of this report, we refer to Visa and MasterCard as card networks. The default interchange rates apply when there are no other interchange fee arrangements in place between an issuer and an acquirer.

[5]Merchants Payments Coalition, Inc. This estimate was calculated using 2006 estimates of a 1.9 percent combined (MasterCard and Visa) average interchange rate and a combined purchase volume of approximately $1.9 trillion.

official travel.[6] GSA negotiates master contracts with card-issuing banks on behalf of federal government entities, which then negotiate agreements with the banks to specify services and requirements for their card programs.

You asked us to review a number of issues concerning interchange fees, including their effect on the federal government—as both an accepter and a user of debit and credit cards—and actions other countries have taken regarding these fees. This report examines (1) the benefits and costs, including interchange fees, associated with federal entities' acceptance of cards as payment for the sale of goods, services, and revenue collection; (2) actions taken in countries that have regulated or otherwise limited interchange fees and their impact; and (3) the impact on federal entities of using cards to make purchases.

To examine the benefits and costs associated with acceptance of cards, we analyzed data representing a broad a range of entities associated with the federal government, including executive, legislative, and judicial branch agencies; government corporations; and other federal instrumentalities that accept credit and debit cards for payment.[7] Card transactions for the majority of executive, judicial, and legislative branch agencies and federal commissions, boards, and other entities are processed by the Department of the Treasury's (Treasury) Financial Management Service (FMS), which pays the associated fees for these entities. We reviewed data on the merchant discount fees FMS paid from fiscal years 2005 through 2007.[8] We also reviewed data from several federal entities for which FMS does not

[6]The cards that government entities use typically are charge cards in which the entire bill must be paid at the end of the billing period, and typically there is no interest.

[7]We use the term "federal entity" throughout this report broadly to refer to departments, agencies, bureaus, government corporations, and any instrumentality or organization that, regardless of whether it receives federally appropriated funds, performs a function sanctioned by the federal government to achieve a federal objective or serve a federal interest. The latter groups of entities include, for example, Amtrak, the U.S. Postal Service, and commercial facilities operated at military bases. Therefore, our estimates of the costs associated with card acceptance by federal entities include some costs that are not directly borne by the government.

[8]Unlike what is done with most merchants, the interchange and other fees paid by FMS on behalf of the federal entities for which it processes card transactions that would constitute the merchant discount fee are not "discounted" from the amount of the card payment. Instead, FMS settles card transactions "at par," and all costs associated with card acceptance are paid separately. For convenience, we use the term "merchant discount fee" throughout this report to refer to the card acceptance fees paid by FMS.

settle transactions: Amtrak, the U.S. Postal Service, and a number of Department of Defense and Department of Homeland Security nonappropriated fund instrumentalities (NAFI), which operate retail stores or recreational facilities for the military.[9] Among the entities included in our review, Amtrak, FMS, and the Postal Service provided data specifically showing the amount of interchange fees paid. For the other entities, we obtained the total amounts paid in merchant discount fees.[10] The data we collected from federal entities were the best data available; however, because of limitations in and differences among the record keeping of the entities, the data may not be complete for all years, may treat some costs inconsistently, and in one case contain estimated, rather than actual, values. We reviewed the data for completeness and accuracy and determined that none of these limitations materially affect the findings we report. (For further information on data sources, as well as a more detailed discussion of our objectives, scope, and methodology, see app. I.) In addition, we reviewed Visa and MasterCard interchange rate tables and met with officials from Visa, MasterCard, American Express, and Discover to obtain information on how these companies determine the rates charged to federal entities. We met with federal entity officials responsible for settling card transactions to identify factors that could affect the interchange rates charged for the transactions. Further, we conducted semistructured interviews with five federal entities for which FMS processes card transactions, based on a selection of entities with the highest and lowest volumes of card transactions.[11] To report on actions taken in countries where interchange rates have been limited by regulation or other means and the effects of those actions, we reviewed available literature, contacted our counterparts (other audit institutions) in several countries, and interviewed officials of the Federal Reserve Bank of Kansas City and industry officials to identify various countries that had addressed interchange rates. To illustrate differing approaches to limiting

[9]NAFIs generally are operated with the proceeds of their activities, rather than with appropriated funds. While these entities do not receive appropriated funds, we included them in our study because they are associated with governmental entities and, to some extent, are controlled by and operated for the benefit of those entities.

[10]We also attempted to collect card acceptance costs from the Smithsonian Institution and from some Coast Guard NAFIs, but the decentralized way in which they maintained their data prevented their providing us with the information.

[11]The federal entities that had high volumes of card acceptance were the Defense Commissary Agency, U.S. Mint, and the Department of Interior's National Park Service. The federal entities that had low volumes of card acceptance were the Corporation for National and Community Service and the National Endowment for the Arts.

interchange rates, we judgmentally selected three countries—Australia, Israel, and Mexico—that adopted diverse approaches and whose efforts had been under way for sufficient time to allow for study. To obtain more detailed information, we conducted literature reviews and interviewed regulators and officials in the three countries. To determine the impact on federal entities of using cards to make purchases, we reviewed policies and procedures developed for the GSA SmartPay program, collected and analyzed data on card use from GSA, and reviewed our prior reports. Finally, we interviewed officials from five entities that were among those with the highest volume of card use in fiscal year 2006 and officials from the bank whose total government card spending was the highest.[12]

We conducted this performance audit from June 2007 to May 2008 in accordance with generally accepted government auditing standards. Those standards require that we plan and perform the audit to obtain sufficient, appropriate evidence to provide a reasonable basis for our findings and conclusions based on our audit objectives. We believe that the evidence obtained provides a reasonable basis for our findings and conclusions based on our audit objectives.

Results in Brief

Federal entities realize various benefits from accepting credit and debit cards, but also incur various costs, including merchant discount and interchange fees, which they are taking steps to control. Federal entity officials told us that the benefits of accepting cards include more satisfied customers, fewer bad checks and cash thefts, and improved operational efficiency. In fiscal year 2007, federal entities collected a total of over $27 billion in revenues through credit and debit card transactions and reported paying at least $433 million in merchant discount fees, which include the interchange fees associated with Visa and MasterCard transactions.[13] The three entities able to separately identify interchange fees—FMS, Amtrak, and the Postal Service—reported that in fiscal year 2007 those fees were about $205 million, out of a total of about $218 million they paid in merchant discount fees for Visa and MasterCard transactions. As card

---

[12]The federal entities that had a high volume of card use were the Department of Agriculture, Department of the Army, Department of Homeland Security, Department of Veterans Affairs, and the U.S. Postal Service.

[13]The fiscal year 2005 through fiscal year 2007 dollar values on the costs and revenues associated with card acceptance are current values and have not been adjusted for inflation.

acceptance has become more common, federal entities have worked to control the associated fees. For example, while the card networks already offer interchange rates for government transactions that are lower than those for many other merchants' transactions, FMS requires its acquiring bank to monitor how transactions are processed to ensure that federal entities' transactions receive the lowest interchange rates for which they are eligible. Some federal entities are working to lower their card acceptance fees by installing equipment needed to accept PIN debit cards, which generally have even lower interchange rates. Also, some federal entities have attempted to negotiate with the card networks to lower interchange rates applicable to their transactions, with varying success. In addition to its efforts focused on card acceptance, FMS initiated a program in 2007 to review the overall efficiency of revenue collection mechanisms used by the federal entities for which it provides services, with a goal of achieving cost savings. As of March 2008, FMS had reviewed eight federal entities under this program and identified potential cost savings and efficiencies at each. Because FMS began this program as a pilot, it has not developed a full implementation strategy. Such a strategy—including a timeline for completing the reviews, estimates for cost savings to be realized, and assessment of the adequacy of resources committed—would help ensure attainment of program goals as expeditiously as possible, as FMS expands the program to other federal entities.

Several countries have taken steps intended to lower interchange rates for a broad range of card transactions within their borders, but complete information on the impact of these actions generally is not available. Among the three countries we examined in more detail, public authorities in Australia and Israel intervened directly to establish limits on the rates that credit card issuers assess for interchange fees on merchant transactions, while in Mexico the association of card-issuing banks voluntarily lowered some interchange rates after a 2004 law gave the Mexican central bank the authority to regulate interchange fees. Research on the impact of the regulation of interchange fees in Australia in 2003 indicates that merchants have likely benefited, as the total merchant discount fees they pay have decreased. However, evidence suggests that the impact on cardholders in that country has been mixed: Australian regulators have not been able to discern whether merchants passed along any reduction in costs to consumers through lower prices. However, issuing banks generally have reduced the rewards offered on reward cards and increased annual and other card fees over the last 5 years. Limited information indicates that merchant discount rates have also declined in Mexico and Israel, but few data on the impact of the actions taken have been published. As the result of differences between the structure and regulation of the U.S. credit and debit card markets and those of other countries, the potential for similar actions to be taken in the United States and the possible impact of such actions are uncertain. For example, the costs associated with issuing cards may be different given the much larger number of issuing banks in the United States than the other countries we studied.

Federal entities obtain numerous benefits when they use cards to make purchases, but also face challenges in minimizing unauthorized or fraudulent use. Card purchases by federal entities totaled more than $27 billion in fiscal year 2007 (a 51 percent rise since fiscal year 1999 after adjusting for inflation), and card usage generally is expected to continue to grow as entities expand the range of items and services that they purchase with cards. For example, some entities have begun using purchase cards to make payments on contracts. Federal entity officials told us that using cards provides a variety of benefits, including lower administrative costs when compared with the slower, more labor-intensive purchasing methods that were previously used. For example, GSA estimated that total administrative cost savings from card use in fiscal year 2006 was $1.7 billion. Further, under the SmartPay program, federal entities obtain rebates of a small percentage of the card purchases that they make from the card-issuing banks; these rebates totaled approximately $175 million in fiscal year 2007. Officials stated that using cards also provides them with enhanced data on purchasing trends, which can be used to negotiate better pricing from vendors. Although receiving various benefits, federal entities using cards to make purchases have had to implement controls and procedures to prevent misuse. Implementing these controls can be challenging; we and others have reported on some entities' inadequate controls over their card programs that have resulted in instances of fraud and abuse. However, officials from some federal entities told us that the risk of fraud and abuse in card programs is less than or equal to that under previously used purchasing methods. Further, some officials told us that tools provided by the issuing banks allow for faster managerial review of transactions and increased capabilities to detect suspicious transactions.

In order to help expeditiously achieve savings to the government, this report recommends that the Secretary of the Treasury take steps to establish a full implementation strategy for FMS's revenue collection review program. Such a strategy should include a timeline for completing the reviews, cost savings estimates associated with individual reviews, and an assessment of the adequacy of the resources committed to the program. In commenting on a draft of this report, the manager of FMS's Internal

Control Branch did not directly address our recommendation, but agreed that the agency's revenue collection review program—which will evaluate the use of credit and debit cards along with other processes—will help improve overall financial management at federal agencies.

Background

As consumers increasingly use credit and debit cards for purchases, federal entities' acceptance of cards to pay for goods and services has also increased. The Treasury's FMS performs the processing for card transactions for executive, judicial, and legislative branch agencies, as well as a number of governmental commissions, boards, and other entities that choose to accept credit and debit cards as a method of payment. Some other federal entities, such as the U.S. Postal Service and Amtrak, operate their own credit and debit card-processing programs and pay the associated fees for processing card transactions. FMS operates the Credit and Debit Card Acquiring Service, a governmentwide service that allows the federal entities for which it collects revenues to accept Visa, MasterCard, American Express, and Discover credit cards, as well as some types of debit cards. The volume of card transactions that FMS processed increased by more than 30 percent from fiscal year 2005 to fiscal year 2007. In fiscal year 2007, FMS processed more than 65 million card payments made to federal entities. FMS pays the fees associated with card acceptance for the federal entities that participate in the Card Acquiring Service.[14]

A merchant—including a government entity—that accepts MasterCard or Visa credit and/or debit cards for payment of goods and services enters into a contract with an acquiring bank that has a relationship with Visa

[14]Unlike private sector entities that pay for these services on their own and can adjust the prices of their goods and services to cover the costs of card acceptance, some federal entities cannot adjust the pricing of their goods and services. For example, the amounts of some U.S. court fees are specified in statute (28 U.S.C. §§1914(a) [Federal Court fee to be paid by party instituting civil proceedings]); similarly, the authorizing statute for the Defense Commissary Agency—which operates grocery stores for military service members and their families—provides that the prices can only be assessed a 5 percent surcharge on top of the cost of the goods. See 10 U.S.C. § 2484(d).

and/or MasterCard to provide card payment-processing services.[15] The merchant contract specifies the level of services the merchant desires, as well as the merchant discount fee and other fees that will apply to the processing of the merchant's card transactions. To provide card acceptance services to federal entities that participate in the Card Acquiring Service, FMS enters into an agreement with a financial institution that has been designated as a financial agent of the U.S. government to provide acquiring banking services. The agreement specifies the services to be provided to FMS and the federal entities that participate in the Card Acquiring Service.[16] Visa and MasterCard establish and enforce rules and standards that may apply to merchants who choose to accept their cards. According to officials of the card networks, however, the networks are not involved in the relationship between a merchant and its acquiring bank.

Fees Allocate the Costs among Parties Associated with Card Transactions

Several parties are involved in a card transaction. For example, Visa and MasterCard transactions involve (1) the bank that issued a cardholder's card, (2) the cardholder, (3) the merchant that accepts the cardholder's card, and (4) an acquiring bank. The acquiring bank charges the merchant a merchant discount fee that is established through negotiations between the merchant and the bank. A portion of the merchant discount fee is generally paid from the acquiring bank to the issuing bank in the form of an interchange fee to cover a portion of the card issuer's costs to issue the card. The balance of the merchant discount fee is retained by the acquiring bank to cover its costs for processing the transaction. A merchant does not pay the interchange fee directly; rather, the interchange fee portion of the merchant discount fee is transferred from the acquiring bank to the issuing bank. Because issuing banks incur costs to issue cards to consumers, the interchange fee helps to allocate these costs among the parties involved in card transactions. Figure 1 illustrates the roles of each

---

[15] In some instances, acquiring banks may contract with third-party entities to provide the card-processing services. In these instances, the third-party entities handle merchant services on behalf of the acquiring bank and may function as a sales agent for an acquirer. A merchant typically establishes a relationship directly with American Express if it wishes to accept this type of card. To accept a Discover card, a merchant may enter into a relationship directly with Discover, or it may enter into a relationship with an acquirer or third-party card processor that has a relationship with Discover.

[16] FMS currently has only one designated financial agent that provides acquiring banking services for the Card Acquiring Service; prior to August 2006, FMS had two designated financial agents that provided acquiring banking services.

of the four parties in a typical credit card transaction and how fees are transferred among the parties.[17] The figure shows that when a cardholder makes a $100 purchase, the merchant pays $2.20 in merchant discount fees for the transaction. This amount is divided between the issuing bank, which receives $1.70 in interchange fees, and the acquiring bank, which receives $0.50 for processing the transaction.

[17]PIN debit and signature debit transactions—in which a cardholder signs a receipt or an electronic screen to authorize the transaction—are processed in a similar manner. In a PIN debit transaction, however, the transaction is routed through the electronic funds transfer network to which the cardholder's depository institution is a member, rather than the Visa or MasterCard network. The transfer of fees associated with both PIN debit and signature debit transactions is the same as a credit card transaction.

Figure 1: Transfer of Fees in a Credit Card Transaction

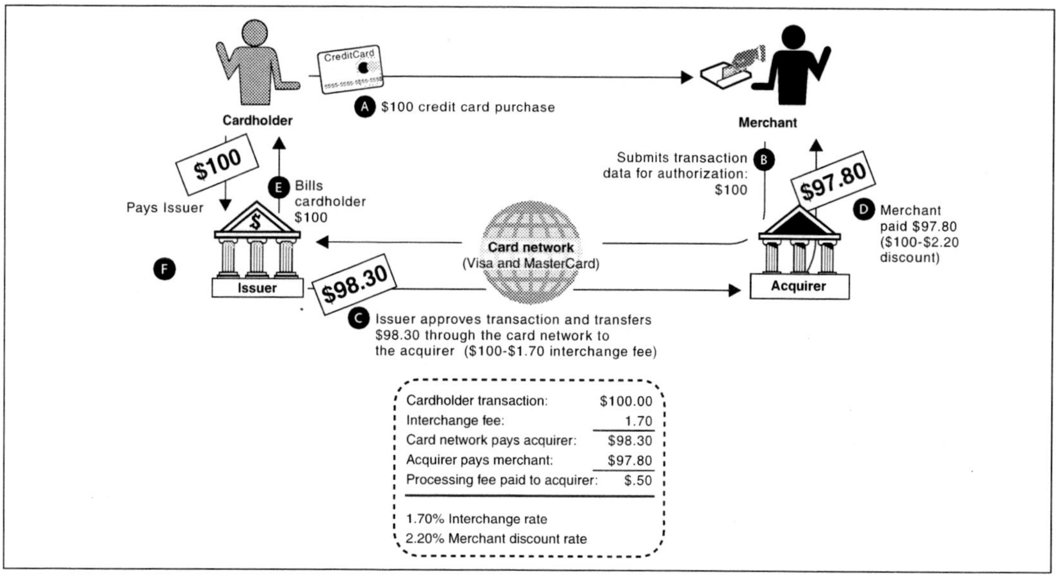

Sources: GAO (analysis); Art Explosion (images).

Note: This is an illustrative example for a typical merchant. The method in which fees are transferred for a federal government entity may differ. For example, for FMS, the interchange and other fees that would constitute the merchant discount fee are not "discounted" from the amount of the card payment. Instead, FMS settles card transactions "at par," and all costs associated with card acceptance are paid separately.

For American Express and Discover card transactions, generally only three parties are involved: the consumer, the merchant, and one company that acts as both the issuing and acquiring entities.[18] Merchants that choose to accept these two types of cards typically negotiate directly with

[18]In the United States, American Express has licensed a number of banks to issue cards on the American Express network; however, it continues to act as the acquiring entity for merchants. Financial arrangements between American Express and third-party bank issuers are agreed upon independently, through separate bilateral agreements, and usually constitute a percentage of the transaction amount. Discover also has card-issuing agreements with financial institutions. For transactions that occur on Discover cards issued by these third-party issuers, Discover receives interchange fees from the acquiring bank and also pays the card issuer an interchange fee.

American Express and Discover over the merchant discount fees that will be assessed on their transactions. Because the issuing and acquiring institution are the same, no interchange fee is involved in the transaction. The merchant discount fees charged on American Express and Discover transactions are, however, set to cover some of the same types of costs that merchant discount fees (which include interchange fees) cover for Visa and MasterCard transactions.

Officials of both the Visa and MasterCard networks told us that they aim to set default interchange rates at a level that encourages banks to issue their cards and merchants to accept those cards. According to the network officials, the rates are set to recognize the value of card acceptance and to reimburse issuing banks for some of the risks and costs incurred in maintaining cardholder accounts, including lending costs, such as the cost of funding the interest-free loan period, the cost associated with cardholders that default on their loans, and losses stemming from fraud. Officials with one of the card networks noted that interchange fees help to reimburse issuers for bearing the costs that merchants would otherwise have to bear for the ability to make sales to customers on credit.

Both Visa and MasterCard develop and publish interchange rate tables that disclose the default rates that apply to various types of transactions. According to Visa and MasterCard officials, four main factors determine interchange rates applicable to a given transaction:

- Type of card—Different interchange rates apply to different types of card products. For example, both MasterCard and Visa have separate interchange rates for general purpose consumer credit cards, reward credit cards, commercial credit cards (issued to businesses), and debit cards. The rates vary because the costs, risks, and revenues associated with these different card products vary for issuers; they also reflect the networks' goal of providing incentives for both issuance and acceptance of cards. For example, reward cards involve higher interchange fees for a number of reasons: According to network officials, such cards tend to provide greater benefits to merchants (in the form of average transaction amounts that are typically higher than those on standard cards) and to cardholders (in the form of cash rebates or points).
- Merchant category—The card networks classify merchants according to the line of business in which they are engaged. Interchange rates may reflect unique characteristics of different merchant categories, such as average profit margins and the way in which merchants authorize transactions. For example, according to card network officials, because

the supermarket industry tends to have very low profit margins, the networks set interchange rates to encourage supermarkets to accept cards. Also, the method in which a merchant authorizes payments can affect the extent to which a card network's system is used. (For example, hotels typically must authorize a payment at least twice—once at guest check-in to ensure the customer is authorized for the minimum payment amount, and again at checkout to authorize the final payment amount.) Additionally, some merchant types may qualify for special incentive interchange rates if a card network determines the merchant category has growth potential for card acceptance. For example, government organizations and utility providers receive lower interchange rates to encourage them to accept cards.

- Merchant size (transaction volume)—Both MasterCard and Visa set lower interchange rates for merchants in some categories that conduct high volumes of card transactions over their networks. For example, according to Visa's default interchange rates that were in effect as of October 2007, supermarkets that conducted a minimum of about 7 million Visa card transactions in calendar year 2006 qualified for lower rates than supermarkets that conducted fewer Visa transactions.

- Mode in which a transaction is processed—Interchange rates also differ depending on how a card transaction is processed. For example, transactions that occur without a card being physically present, such as in Internet transactions, carry a greater risk of fraud; therefore, higher interchange rates apply to these transactions. Similarly, swiping a card through a card terminal, rather than key-entering the account number, provides more information to the issuing bank to verify the validity of a transaction; therefore, swipe transactions are assessed a lower interchange rate.

Interchange Fees Are Not Directly Regulated, but Are the Subject of Legislative Initiatives and Litigation

Interchange fees are not regulated at the federal level in the United States. The Federal Reserve, under the Truth in Lending Act (TILA), however, is responsible for creating and enforcing requirements relating to the disclosure of terms and conditions of consumer credit, including those applicable to credit cards.[19] In addition, the Federal Reserve and other federal agencies, including the Office of the Comptroller of the Currency,

[19]Pub. L. No. 90-321, Title I, 82 Stat. 146 (1968) (codified as amended at 15 U.S.C. §§ 1601-1666). See GAO, *Credit Cards: Increased Complexity in Rates and Fees Heightens Need for More Effective Disclosures to Consumers*, GAO-06-929 (Washington, D.C.: Sept. 12, 2006).

the Federal Deposit Insurance Corporation, the Office of Thrift Supervision, and the National Credit Union Administration oversee credit card issuers. As part of their oversight, these regulators review card issuers' compliance with TILA and ensure that an institution's credit card operations do not pose a threat to the institution's safety and soundness. The Federal Trade Commission (FTC) generally has responsibility for enforcing TILA and other consumer protection laws for credit card issuers that are not depository institutions.

As of early 2008, interchange fees were the subject of federal and state legislative proposals. For example, the Credit Card Fair Fee Act of 2008, introduced in March 2008, would, according to one of the bill's sponsors, establish a process by which merchants and issuing banks could agree to set interchange fees and other terms of access to covered electronic payments systems without violating federal antitrust laws. Additionally, the bill would establish a three-judge panel, called the "Electronic Payment System Judges," to make determinations of access rates and terms for electronic payments systems. The purpose of the panel would be to conduct proceedings to ensure that the rates and terms established by participants in the system are calculated to represent the rates and terms that would be negotiated in a perfectly competitive marketplace, that is, a marketplace of willing buyers and sellers in which neither has market power. [20] Also, under legislative initiatives pending in some states, merchants who are parties to payment card agreements would be given access to information about the issuing bank's interchange fees, including a schedule of all interchange fees charged by the bank, as well as notice of any change in the fees.[21] State bills also would, among other things,

- prohibit a financial institution that issues a credit card or debit card from charging any fee, including interchange fees, based on the sales and use tax portion of a retail sales transaction.[22]

- prohibit a financial institution from increasing the fee based on the size or cost of a transaction.[23]

[20] H.R. 5546, 110th Cong. (2008).

[21] See, e.g., H.B. 2857, 82nd Leg., (KS 2008); L.B 174, 100th Leg., (NE 2007); A.B. 7775, NY 2007-2008 Regular Sess. (2007).

[22] S.B. 1138, 213th Leg. (NJ 2008); H.B. 3321 51st Leg., 2d Sess. (OK 2008).

[23] See, e.g., H.B. 2856, 82nd Leg. (KS 2008).

- call on Congress to assess the impact on merchants of interchange fees and other discount fees and to require credit card issuers to be more open with merchants about the costs of the payment systems in which they participate.[24]

As of March 2008, none of the initiatives had been enacted into law.

Interchange fees also have been a factor in lawsuits alleging violations of the antitrust laws by credit card networks and related parties.[25] The plaintiffs in those cases alleged that interchange fees were an example of the networks' unlawful exercise of market power. As of October 2005, merchants had instituted at least 14 class action lawsuits in four separate districts against Visa and MasterCard and their member banks, alleging specifically that the defendants fixed interchange fees at supracompetitive levels in violation of Section One of the Sherman Antitrust Act.[26] Currently, in a consolidated action pending in the United States District Court for the Eastern District of New York, merchants claim that interchange fees have an anticompetitive effect in violation of the federal antitrust laws.[27] Appendix II provides additional information on cases that include, among other things, allegations that interchange rates were a function of anticompetitive conduct in violation of antitrust laws.

Government Entities Also Use Cards

Under GSA's SmartPay program, GSA negotiates master contracts with banks to issue cards to federal entities that participate in the program. The first SmartPay master contracts were established in 1998 with five banks.

[24]Sen. J. Mem. Res. 8020, 60th First Reg. Sess. (WA 2007); H.J.R. 53 (VT. 2008).

[25]These include cases involving allegations that interchange fees are evidence of the use of market power to commit unlawful price fixing and tying. See, e.g., In re Visa Check/Mastermoney Antitrust Litig., 297 F. Supp. 2d 503 (E.D.N.Y. 2003) (Wal-Mart I), aff'd sub nom., *Wal-Mart Stores, Inc. v. Visa USA, Inc.*, 396 F.3d 96 (2d Cir. 2005) (Wal-Mart II); see also *United States v. Visa U.S.A., Inc.*, 163 F . Supp. 2d . 322 (S.D.N.Y. 2001), *aff'd*, 344 F.3d 229 (2d Cir 2003), *dert. Denied*, 543 U.S. 811 (2004).

[26]15 U.S.C. §§ 1 – 7.

[27]In re Payment Card Interchange Fee and Merchant Discount Antitrust Litigation, 398 F. Supp.2d 1356 (MDL Oct. 19, 2005). According to the Magistrate Judge assigned to the case, as of February 2006 "some forty class action lawsuits" had been brought "on behalf of a class of merchants against the defendant credit card networks and certain of their member banks." In re Payment Card Interchange Fee and Merchant Discount Antitrust Litigation, 2006 U.S. Dist. LEXIS 45727; 2006-1 Trade Cas. (CCH) P75,278 (E.D.N.Y.) As of March 2008, the action remained in pretrial proceedings.

These contracts are set to expire in November 2008 and will be replaced by new master contracts with four issuing banks under GSA's SmartPay 2 program. Participating federal entities choose a bank from among those under contract with GSA that offer services that meet their needs, and develop individual task orders that specify the products and services that the banks will provide them. In negotiating their individual task orders, these federal entities also can specify to the issuing banks other services they may need to operate their card programs. For example, banks can provide tools that the federal entities use to monitor card usage and expenses, or customer service support, such as 24-hour emergency card service for federal employees.

Federal Entities Are Taking Steps to Control Cost Realizing the Benefits Associated with Accepting Credit and Debit Cards

Federal entities realize benefits from accepting credit and debit cards, including increased customer satisfaction, fewer bad checks and cash thefts, and improved operational efficiency. Realizing these benefits entails costs, principally the merchant discount fees associated with card transactions but also the costs for related equipment needed to process the transactions. In fiscal year 2007, federal entities from which we collected data reported paying $433 million dollars in merchant discount fees for the processing of over $27 billion in credit and debit card revenues. As card acceptance has become more common, federal entities have worked to control the associated fees, including reviewing the ways in which transactions are processed to ensure they qualify for the lowest possible interchange rates. Additionally, FMS began a pilot program in which it is reviewing the revenue collection mechanisms of the federal entities for which it provides services, with the aim of identifying cost savings and efficiencies. FMS has reviewed collection cash flows for eight federal entities thus far and has identified cost-savings opportunities. While it plans to conduct over 100 more reviews, it has not yet developed a full implementation strategy for the program. Such a strategy would help ensure that FMS achieves the program's goals as expeditiously as possible and increase overall savings to the government.

Federal Entities Receive Numerous Benefits Associated with Card Acceptance

The ability to accept credit and debit cards provides a variety of benefits to federal entities, including greater customer satisfaction and improved internal operations. Officials at several federal entities noted that card acceptance helped to ensure that the federal entities would remain competitive with private sector organizations. Many of the officials we spoke with told us that consumers expect to be able to use cards to make payments, and some stated that they did not think they could stop accepting cards. For example, Amtrak officials stated that customers paying with cards account for about 85 percent of its sales and that if they did not accept cards, the number of people who ride their trains would decline significantly. Among the benefits mentioned by federal officials with whom we spoke was that card acceptance improves customer satisfaction with their organizations because consumers like to use their cards for convenience, credit card reward programs, and security reasons. Accepting cards also has enabled entities to conduct business via the Internet, which can reduce labor costs associated with sales and also can provide greater convenience to customers. For example, officials from the U.S. Mint stated that about 50 percent of their sales occurred through the Mint's Web site. Some entities also stated that the ability to accept cards has increased their sales volume.

Federal entity officials also noted that accepting cards reduces the amount spent on processing other forms of payment. By accepting cards, federal entities incurred less expense in transporting cash, lower losses from theft of cash, and had fewer bad check expenses. For example, officials at the Department of the Interior noted that cash transport costs can be high for some remote parks and wildlife refuges. Several federal officials also stated that accepting cards has reduced the costs associated with processing checks, and that funds are deposited in accounts faster when customers use credit or debit cards than when they use checks. Additionally, Amtrak officials told us that accepting cards onboard trains for ticket and food and beverage sales resulted in fewer instances of employee theft of cash.

Finally, many officials cited that card acceptance improved internal operations at their entities. For example, officials at the Department of the Interior stated that payments made by credit cards result in a more streamlined bookkeeping approach because card sales involve less paperwork (for reconciliation) than other payment forms. Defense Commissary Agency (DeCA) officials also stated that they believed that labor associated with reconciling sales at the end of the day declined as a result of the reduced volume of cash. Additional operational efficiencies mentioned by officials included a reduction in costs and exposure to fraud and errors from misplacing or miscounting cash and checks. Some officials stated that the efficiencies gained in their internal operations as a result of card acceptance allowed them to reallocate staff to different and more productive uses. For example, officials at the Department of the Interior explained that card acceptance at automated kiosks allowed them to reallocate some staff that used to collect entrance fees to more productive tasks. Amtrak officials also stated that customers' ability to purchase tickets using cards, especially through the Amtrak Web site, has reduced their labor costs.

Because the federal entities that utilize FMS's collection services are not responsible for the associated card-processing costs, we could not determine how officials at these agencies would regard card acceptance if they had to pay these costs. However, an official at one federal entity that accepts cards and pays the associated costs noted that it is difficult to assess if the savings from receiving less revenue in the form of cash or checks (and more from cards) sufficiently offsets the entity's card-related processing costs, including the interchange fees. He also stated that it is uncertain whether the entity receives higher revenues from accepting cards, as some customers would likely spend the same amount with them regardless of the type of payment used. However, customers demand convenient payment alternatives, and for some of their products, private sector entities provide similar services, and thus he believed the ability to accept cards allows the entity to stay competitive with these entities.

The federal entities we contacted were not able to provide comprehensive data on any cost savings from accepting cards. We identified various government, academic, and industry studies that compared the cost of processing for different forms of payment; however, many of these studies found that precise estimates were difficult to calculate. Additionally, while most of the studies we reviewed found cash to be the least expensive payment form to process, the methodologies used in the studies were not consistent and the data contained in many of them were outdated.[28]

As Card Revenues Have Increased, So Have Associated Costs

The volume of revenues accepted through credit and debit card payments was growing for the group of federal entities we reviewed. Data on revenues collected by FMS, which processes the card transactions for a large number of federal executive, legislative, and judicial branch agencies and other federal entities, show that while credit and debit card

---

[28]David B. Humphrey and Allen N. Berger. 1990. "Market Failure and Resource Use: Economic Incentives to Use Different Payment Instruments." In *The U.S. Payment System: Efficiency, Risk and the Role of the Federal Reserve: Proceedings of a Symposium on the U.S. Payment System Sponsored by the Federal Reserve Bank of Richmond*, ed. David B. Humphrey, pp. 45-86. Boston: Kluwer Academic Publishers. D. D. Garcia-Swartz, R. W. Hahn, and A. Layne-Farrar, "The Move Toward a Cashless Society: Calculating the Costs and Benefits," *Review of Network Economics*, vol. 5, no. 2 (2006). D. Humphrey, M. Willesson, T. Lindblom, and G. Bergendahl, "What Does It Cost to Make a Payment," *Review of Network Economics*, vol. 2, no. 2, (2003).

transactions accounted for only 0.23 percent of the total federal government revenues FMS collected in fiscal year 2007, its card collections have grown by almost 28 percent in just 2 years—from approximately $5.5 billion in fiscal year 2005 to almost $7.1 billion in fiscal year 2007 (in current dollars). As shown in table 1, the other federal entities from which we collected data also experienced an increase in card payments over the 3-year period, with the total reaching approximately $27 billion in credit and debit transactions for fiscal year 2007.[29] (App. I contains a detailed discussion of our data sources and analysis of the data reported to us from the federal entities.)

Table 1: Credit and Debit Card Revenues Collected and Merchant Discount Fees Paid by Federal Entities, Fiscal Years 2005–

(in current dollars)

2007 Fiscal year	Entity	Credit and debit card revenues collected (dollars in billions)	Merchant discount fees paid[a] (dollars in millions)	Average merchant discount rate
2005	Financial Management Service	$5.5	$70	1.26%
	NAFIs (all)	7.5	128	1.72
	U.S. Postal Service and Amtrak	9.3	143	1.54
	Total	**22.3**	**341**	**1.53**
2006	Financial Management Service	6.3	89	1.41
	NAFIs (all)	8.3	139	1.67
	U.S. Postal Service and Amtrak	10.4	160	1.54
	Total	**25.0**	**387**	**1.55**
2007	Financial Management Service	7.1	101	1.43
	NAFIs (all)	8.5	150	1.75
	U.S. Postal Service and Amtrak	11.5	182	1.58
	Total	**$27.1**	**$433**	**1.60%**

Source: GAO analysis of federal entity data.

Source: GAO analysis of federal entity data.

Note: Not all entities from which we collected data operate on the federal fiscal year of October 1 through September 30; therefore, the data presented for fiscal years represent some costs associated with dates that fall outside of the federal fiscal year.

[a]We use the term "merchant discount fee" throughout this report to refer to the card acceptance fees paid by federal entities. For FMS, the merchant discount fees are not "discounted" from the amount of the card payment. Instead, FMS settles card transactions "at par," and all costs associated with card acceptance are paid separately.

[29]Not all entities from which we collected data operate on the federal fiscal year of October 1 through September 30; therefore, the data presented for fiscal years represent some costs associated with dates that fall outside of the federal fiscal year.

As revenues from card payments have increased, so has the total amount of merchant discount fees paid by the federal entities from which we collected data. These federal entities reported paying a total of almost $433 million in merchant discount fees in fiscal year 2007 (see table 1). This figure represents an almost 12 percent increase over the amount paid in fiscal year 2006 and an almost 27 percent increase over the amount paid in fiscal year 2005. The average merchant discount rate increased about 4 percent from fiscal year 2005 to fiscal year 2007.

Among the entities included in our review, Amtrak, FMS, and the Postal Service provided data specifically showing the amount of interchange fees associated with their Visa and MasterCard transactions (their acquiring banks provide them with these data). These three entities paid a total of approximately $205 million in interchange fees during fiscal year 2007, out of a total $218 million in merchant discount fees specifically for MasterCard and Visa transactions.[30] These interchange fees accounted for the majority of total merchant discount fees these entities paid for accepting all card types. As card revenues and merchant discount fees increased for these three entities, so did the interchange fees they paid. Interchange fees increased by almost 36 percent, from almost $151 million in fiscal year 2005 to $205 million in fiscal year 2007 (in fiscal year 2006, they were $179 million).

For a variety of reasons, some of the Department of Defense and Department of Homeland Security NAFIs were not able to separate interchange fees from the total merchant discount fees they paid. (For example, according to an official from one entity, its contract with its acquiring bank specified that all credit card transactions would be charged a fixed percentage fee, regardless of the interchange fees associated with a particular transaction; therefore, the entity did not have specific information on interchange fees.) The data provided by these entities showed that both card revenues and the associated merchant discount fees increased over the 2005 to 2007 period. Revenues from sales made on cards were about $7.5 billion in fiscal year 2005 and over $8.5 billion in

[30]This estimate for interchange fees paid includes fees associated with PIN debit transactions as well as MasterCard and Visa credit and signature debit transactions. We were not able to determine the portion of the PIN debit interchange fees that were specifically paid for Visa and MasterCard PIN debit transactions. It is possible that some of the PIN debit transactions reported by these entities were routed through other debit networks and, therefore, are not necessarily Visa and MasterCard transactions. Also, some federal entities included quarterly fees paid to Visa and MasterCard in the interchange fees figures they reported; therefore, our estimated interchange fee amount includes these fees.

fiscal year 2007, an approximately 14 percent increase. The merchant discount fees for card payments at these entities also increased from approximately $128 million in fiscal year 2005 to almost $150 million in fiscal year 2007, an increase of almost 17 percent.

For some payments made using cards, the government does not bear merchant discount costs.[31] For example, consumers can pay their income and business taxes to the Internal Revenue Service (IRS) using cards. To accept these payments, IRS has agreements with two private third-party entities that process payments for individuals or businesses that choose to use a credit or debit card to make a tax payment. The two private entities charge a convenience fee of 2.49 percent of the total tax payment for taxpayers who use their services, a portion of which covers the merchant discount fees paid by the third-party entity to its acquiring bank.[32] In fiscal year 2007, these merchant discount fees totaled about $47.5 million for approximately $2.4 billion in tax payments, an 85 percent increase in tax payments made with credit and debit cards from fiscal year 2005.

In addition to the interchange and processing fees that make up the merchant discount fee, federal entities face other costs associated with the acceptance of credit and debit cards. For example, entities must pay for equipment and software for card transactions, such as point-of-sale terminals, keypads for PIN debit card transactions, computers, modems, and printers, and pay for their installation and maintenance. While FMS pays the merchant discount fees associated with card transactions for entities for which it settles transactions, it does not pay for the costs associated with equipment and software; these costs are the responsibility of the entities. Other costs of accepting cards include complying with industry security standards, known as the Payment Card Industry Data Security Standard, training employees to process and reconcile card transactions, and experiencing losses associated with fraudulent use of cards. However, information provided by some entities indicated that

[31]We did not include such transactions in compiling the total merchant discount fees paid by federal entities for card acceptance. Instead, we provide this information as an example of additional fees that are paid by consumers for card acceptance associated with government payments.

[32]This fee also applies to debit card payments in which the taxpayer does not enter a PIN to authorize the transaction. Beginning in the 2008 tax season, both third-party entities will have implemented PIN-less debit capabilities in which a customer's card number will be recognized as a debit card and routed through the appropriate card network for a flat fee of $2.95.

these additional costs were not significant compared to merchant discount fees.

Federal Entities Are Making Efforts to Reduce Card Acceptance Costs

As card acceptance has grown, federal entities have used several methods to manage their costs and reduce the fees associated with card transactions. One method is to ensure that their Visa and MasterCard transactions are processed so as to qualify for the lowest applicable interchange rate. Both Visa and MasterCard have a merchant category for federal entities, and the interchange rates for the transactions of merchants in these categories are lower than those for many other merchant categories.[33] As long as federal entities' transactions meet all applicable processing requirements—for example, they must be submitted for final settlement in a timely manner—the entities are charged the interchange rate applicable to those merchant categories. For example, as of April 2008, if transactions met all applicable processing requirements, government entities accepting a MasterCard consumer credit card as payment would pay an interchange fee of 1.55 percent of the transaction amount plus $0.10, and if accepting a Visa consumer credit card, an interchange fee of 1.43 percent of the transaction amount plus $0.05.[34] (In comparison, the interchange rate applicable to a MasterCard general purpose consumer credit card transaction at some fast food stores is 1.90 percent.) In some cases, card transactions at federal entities can be assessed a lower rate. For example, FMS officials told us that the DeCA's transactions qualify to be processed using the interchange rate applicable to the supermarket merchant category, which can range from 1.27 percent to 1.48 percent plus $0.05 for MasterCard general purpose consumer credit card transactions, depending on the volume of card transactions processed.

Given that the method in which the card is accepted, transaction volume, and other factors can affect interchange rates, many federal entities have taken steps to ensure that the acceptance and processing procedures they follow result in the most advantageous interchange rates applying to their transactions. For example, Amtrak officials explained that by replacing card machines (that embossed paper receipts) with wireless card

[33]This category is referred to as Public Sector for MasterCard and Customer Payment Service Retail 2 (Emerging Markets) for Visa.

[34]Different interchange rates may apply when a commercial card is presented for payment at a federal entity.

terminals on trains, they were able to significantly reduce the interchange rates that applied to transactions made aboard their trains, because the electronic transaction qualified for a lower interchange rate than the paper transactions.

Moreover, FMS officials explained that before the agency signed the current agreement with their acquiring bank in August 2006, they carefully reviewed the bank's interchange management capabilities and incorporated provisions to ensure that the bank employs them. For example, the bank is responsible for monitoring how card transactions are being processed and the interchange rates they are being assessed. In addition, the bank provides FMS with daily and monthly reports that provide various levels of detail on the interchange fees paid. Both the bank and FMS officials review these reports to identify instances in which transactions may have been charged a higher interchange rate—known as a downgrade—because they were not processed under the requirements necessary to qualify for a lower rate. An FMS official stated that FMS then works with the acquiring bank and individual federal entity that processed the transaction to identify the reasons and to resolve the problem in order to avoid future downgrades. For example, an FMS official explained that in one instance a DeCA store had a broken card terminal in a checkout aisle that prevented employees from swiping cards. Instead, employees keyed in card information, which resulted in a number of transactions being downgraded and assessed a higher interchange rate. With the assistance of FMS's acquiring bank, the problem was identified and DeCA employees were told that should the problem reoccur, they are to use other terminals to process card transactions, which would ensure they would not be assessed a higher rate. An FMS official stated that under the current agreement with its acquiring bank, very few transactions have been downgraded; however, FMS still works to resolve these instances when they occur so that the total cost associated with government transactions can be reduced. Officials of two other federal government entities told us that they similarly review data provided by their acquiring banks to identify opportunities to reduce fees.

Another way that several federal entities have attempted to control fees associated with card acceptance is by expanding their ability to accept PIN debit card payments. For example, PIN debit transactions generally are assessed lower interchange rates than "signature" debits, and therefore some federal entities are beginning to implement the technology necessary to accept these transactions. While federal entities must make an investment in the equipment needed to process PIN debit transactions (for example, PIN pads), one entity told us that the much lower interchange rates associated with PIN debit transactions justified the investment. An FMS official stated that the only entity for which it processes card transactions that currently has the ability to accept PIN debit cards is DeCA; however, as entities undergo equipment upgrades, FMS works with them to identify equipment that may lower overall collection costs. For example, one federal entity is in the process of developing a new terminal system for card collections, and as part of this process, FMS is encouraging the entity to implement a system that has the capability to process PIN debit transactions. Additionally, some of the military NAFIs with which we spoke adopted technologies necessary to accept PIN debit cards, stating that they too recognized the cost savings associated with these transactions.

Federal entities also can reduce card acceptance fees by changing the way in which they or their acquiring banks connect to various card networks. For example, Postal Service officials explained that they were in the process of converting to a new method of processing transactions called a payment switch, which will funnel all of the information from the Postal Service's 70,000 terminals into one settlement file at the end of the day. The file then is sent to a third-party card processor. The officials explained that the payment switch will reduce substantially the processing fee component of card payment costs, because the technology in the payment switch allows for routing each transaction to the lowest cost processor. Additionally, the payment switch will enable the Postal Service to send some card transactions directly to a card company rather than through the third-party processor, reducing the cost of accepting those transactions. FMS's current acquiring bank has also implemented changes in the method by which it processes PIN debit card transactions. FMS officials explained that the bank identified a method for routing PIN debit card transactions to different networks so that the costs for processing the transaction are minimized, resulting in annual savings of almost $300,000 for FMS.

Federal Entities Have Attempted to Negotiate Lower Fees

Another way in which federal entities have acted to reduce card acceptance costs is by negotiating with their acquiring banks for lower merchant discount rates or with card networks for lower interchange rates. Some of the federal entities we reviewed have realized card acceptance savings by negotiating new acquiring bank services contracts. These entities were able to negotiate lower rates for the processing component of the merchant discount rate applied to their transactions. For example, by signing a new acquiring bank agreement, one federal entity received a substantial reduction in the processing fee component of its merchant discount rate. Also, to obtain a more favorable merchant discount rate for their transactions, officials from some of the military service NAFIs have been working together to try to negotiate a lower merchant discount rate with American Express on the basis of the volume of transactions they provide to that company.

Officials at some of the entities with whom we spoke stated that they did not believe they could negotiate effectively with the card networks—MasterCard and Visa—for lower interchange rates for their transactions. However, some federal entities stated that they have attempted to negotiate and have had varying levels of success:

- FMS officials told us that they tried to negotiate lower interchange rates with both Visa and MasterCard by stating that some factors that are included in determining interchange rates do not necessarily apply to federal government transactions. For example, FMS officials argued that the federal entities that participate in the Card Acquiring Service pose less risk than other merchant types and that there is no risk of delinquency on the part of the Treasury. FMS officials stated that their negotiations were not successful and that they were not able to negotiate lower interchange rates.

- Officials from the Postal Service also explained their attempts to negotiate with the card networks. They stated that they believe lower interchange rates should be applied to their transactions for a variety of reasons. First, the Postal Service estimates that it is one of the top U.S. merchants in terms of card transaction volume. Second, there is less risk of fraud than some other merchants because most transactions are conducted face to face. Third, the Postal Service operates a large retail network with 35,000 offices, self-service terminals, mail and phone orders, plus a Web site that receives approximately 30 million hits per month and provides a great amount of visibility for the networks. Fourth, the Postal Service has its own law enforcement agency that investigates instances of fraud, including fraudulent use of cards where merchandise travels through the mail. These investigations result in the recovery of merchandise as well as stolen card data and in some cases the arrest of international criminals to the benefit of the credit card industry. They noted that the benefit of such a service to the card networks was not reflected in the interchange rates applicable to Postal Service transactions. The officials did state that they have had some limited success in negotiations with the card networks resulting in some small cost savings.

- Officials from another federal entity told us that they have had some success in receiving funds from one of the networks as a result of a joint marketing program. The funds could be used to reduce interchange costs and/or for additional marketing efforts; however, the details of the negotiations are bound by confidentiality agreements and are considered proprietary information. The officials explained that negotiations of this type are not typical of federal entities because of the limited marketing opportunities available to most government entities.

Although some federal entities have had some success in negotiating lower interchange rates for their transactions, whether additional opportunities exist for further reductions in interchange rates is unclear. According to officials of MasterCard and Visa, among the factors that are considered when setting interchange rates is whether the industry or sector represents a new market for credit and debit cards. According to these officials, they see government payments as a market in which they hope to increase card acceptance and transaction volumes; thus, the interchange rates that Visa and MasterCard set for government transactions are lower than those of many other merchant categories. Additionally, officials at both MasterCard and Visa told us that opportunities exist for merchants, including federal entities, to negotiate for lower interchange rates assessed on their transactions. For example, the MasterCard officials explained an instance in which, in response to rapidly rising gasoline prices, they worked with gasoline merchants to develop a cap on the interchange fees that can be charged on petroleum purchases. Officials from both networks explained that they have individuals dedicated to developing customized arrangements with merchants and that these negotiations involve identifying mutually beneficial arrangements for both the merchant and the network. Also, we found it difficult to assess whether federal entities could negotiate rate reductions based on their relative transaction volume or aggregate card revenues, because we could not identify any publicly available data we could use to determine how the federal government's total transaction volume or aggregate card revenues compare with those of other large merchants.

FMS Has Begun a Program to Identify Cost Savings Opportunities, but Has Yet to Develop a Full Implementation Strategy

In addition to looking for opportunities to reduce card acceptance costs, FMS has initiated a program to review the overall cash management practices of federal entities. In its role as the federal government's central collection services provider, FMS provides federal entities with a number of alternative revenue collection mechanisms to meet their needs. It is also responsible for ensuring that the federal government's collection activities are efficient and that costs are minimized. Additionally, according to FMS, the Deficit Reduction Act of 1984 authorizes FMS to conduct periodic cash management reviews of federal entities' financial operations.[35] In the past, FMS allowed federal entities for which it collected revenues to pick from the variety of collection mechanisms that FMS offered without examining the most cost-efficient mechanisms of collecting the revenue. However, the Office of Management and Budget's (OMB) 2004 assessment of FMS's collections program identified the need for FMS to develop additional techniques to convince the federal entities to reduce paper-based collections.

In 2007, FMS piloted a program to review the revenue collection mechanisms used by the federal entities for which it collects revenues, and how and from whom payments to these entities typically are made. The reviews are designed to identify inefficiencies in current collection mechanisms and to help FMS attain one of its strategic goals of providing timely collection of federal government revenues, at the lowest cost, through electronic means. According to FMS officials, the program is not focused on card transactions, but rather on overall payment management improvements. The reviews will allow FMS to work with federal entities to take advantage of advances in lower-cost technology that may have occurred since the entities began using their existing mechanisms. Among other things, FMS is examining whether entities are using paper collection mechanisms when they could instead be using electronic mechanisms, or—if electronic mechanisms are already being used—opportunities to reduce any associated fees by substituting cheaper electronic mechanisms. For example, if an entity accepts credit cards, FMS may also suggest cheaper collection alternatives, such as PIN debit cards or automated clearinghouse transactions.[36] Once it has reviewed an entity's collections and processes and identified improvements, FMS develops an agreement that details the changes to be made and the timeline for implementing them. FMS officials explained that while entities are not mandated to implement changes in their collection mechanisms, the

[35]Pub. L. No. 98-369 § 2652, 31 U.S.C. § 3720; see also 31 C.F.R. Part 206 and Department of the Treasury, Financial Management Service, *Cash Management Made Easy* (Washington, D.C., 2002). These reviews examine and analyze agency management of the following programs: collections and deposits, disbursements, inventories, imprest funds (such as petty cash funds), and other cash held outside the Treasury. The federal entity and FMS agree on any recommendations from these reviews and on plans for improvement.

[36]The automated clearinghouse is a processing and delivery system that provides for the distribution and settlement of electronic financial transactions. Debits and credits are cleared electronically, rather than through the physical movement of checks or cash.

agreements will provide for an "inefficiency charge" that will assess penalties to the entity if the agreed-upon recommendations are not implemented by the dates stipulated in the agreement. Such charges will be calculated on a per transaction basis and require that the entity transfer funds to the Treasury to cover the amount.

In determining which entities to review for the pilot phase, FMS officials said that their focus for the program was first on the 24 Chief Financial Officer (CFO) agencies identified in the Chief Financial Officers Act of 1990.[37] FMS officials said that they also focused on entities that showed the most potential for savings that could be realized by revising their collection mechanisms. Criteria used for selecting agencies to participate in the pilot program included (1) the dollar volume of the entity's collections, (2) the amount of revenue not collected in electronic form (that is, cash and checks), and (3) entities with whom FMS previously experienced good cooperation in converting paper processes to electronic mechanisms.

As of March 2008, FMS had reviewed collection cash flows at eight federal entities and had drafted agreements to implement revised collection procedures with each.[38] The results confirm that opportunities for improvement exist, although only two of the eight agreements have been signed (the agency's goal for the program for fiscal year 2008 is to have at least six of the eight agreements signed). Through the eight agreements that have been developed, FMS has identified various potential process improvements and changes that would result in recurring cost savings. For

[37]See 31 U.S.C. § 901(b). The agencies listed in this provision are the Departments of Agriculture, Commerce, Defense, Education, Energy, Health and Human Services, Homeland Security, Housing and Urban Development, the Interior, Justice, Labor, State, Transportation, the Treasury, Veterans Affairs, and the Environmental Protection Agency, the National Aeronautics and Space Administration, the Agency for International Development, the General Services Administration, the National Science Foundation, the Nuclear Regulatory Commission, the Office of Personnel Management, the Small Business Administration, and the Social Security Administration.

[38]The eight entities ranged from individual agencies or bureaus to entire federal departments, due to differences in the complexity of entities' revenue streams. The entities that participated in the pilot included the Department of Agriculture—Forest Service, Department of Defense—Defense Commissary Agency, Department of Education—Federal Student Aid and Administrative Office; Department of Homeland Security—Customs and Border Protection; Department of Housing and Urban Development; Department of the Treasury—Internal Revenue Service; Department of Labor—Employment and Training Administration and Employment Standards Administration; and National Aeronautics and Space Administration.

example, FMS staff determined that replacing the check-processing method DeCA used with a more advanced method that converts paper checks to electronic images at the point of sale would produce savings each time a check is presented at a DeCA location. FMS officials told us that they previously had developed a general estimate for cost savings that could be achieved by converting from paper collection mechanisms to electronic collection mechanisms before beginning the program; however, they have not developed cost savings estimates that would be achieved by implementing the specific actions that they have recommended at each of the entities they have reviewed thus far. At our request, FMS officials developed an estimate of the cost savings associated with a recommendation contained in one of the draft agreements they have prepared. FMS estimated that if IRS converted 67 million payments currently being received in paper to transactions processed by an electronic system, savings of approximately $40 million annually would result.

FMS officials stated that they have begun to prioritize the order in which they will conduct reviews for the remainder of the federal entities. They estimate that they will conduct reviews, and draft agreements, with as many as 85 entities within the 24 CFO agencies. An FMS official estimated that the average length of the reviews they plan to complete should take approximately 6 to 9 months; however, each of the reviews that have been conducted as part of the pilot have taken longer. FMS officials attributed the extra length of time to conduct reviews during the pilot phase to the fact that the program is new, and they have spent time developing a standard review process and templates for the agreements. Additionally, the officials explained that much of the success and length of time a review takes is dependent on the willingness of the entities to work with FMS and to incorporate the recommended changes into their existing mission and goals. After reviews of the CFO agencies are completed, FMS officials anticipate that an additional 29 reviews will be conducted for the non-CFO agencies for which FMS provides collection services. The FMS staff responsible for conducting these reviews consists of five full-time staff members that constitute a new customer relationship management group formed in the last few years, and performing the reviews currently consumes the majority of these staff members' time. In addition to these five staff members, FMS has a director who oversees the program, as well as staff in various program areas within FMS that assist in different stages of the reviews.

Because FMS began this program as a pilot, it has not developed a full implementation strategy that could help ensure an appropriate resource commitment and timely attainment of its goals. For example, FMS officials told us they have not developed a timeline for completion of the reviews for all agencies because they are focused on the 24 CFO agencies. However, because this program will help FMS achieve its strategic goal of increasing the percentage of federal government revenues collected electronically—a percentage that has remained constant for the last 3 fiscal years—establishing a targeted timeline for completing the remaining reviews could help FMS ensure that it makes progress toward this goal. In addition, in its 2004 review, OMB noted that FMS lacked policies and techniques for convincing federal entities to eliminate paper-based collections. Including in its reviews estimates of the cost savings to be achieved by implementing the recommended changes could help FMS emphasize to the entities the importance of acting on the recommendations that it identifies. Finally, FMS has already found that reviews are taking more time to complete than it initially anticipated. The cost savings associated with implementing the efficiencies identified in the reviews are both immediate and recurring. Accordingly, as the pilot program is fully implemented, ensuring that it has adequate resources for completing the reviews expeditiously would help achieve the program's goals.

Other Countries Have Acted to Influence Interchange Rates, but Limited Information Is Available on the Effects of These Actions on Consumers

Authorities in as many as 26 countries have taken or considered actions intended to either limit interchange fees or improve card payment systems. In the 3 countries we examined in more detail—Australia, Israel, and Mexico—reforms designed to effect reductions in interchange rates were undertaken as part of broader efforts to change payment systems or card markets; thus, isolating the effects of the interchange interventions is difficult. Further, differences regarding the regulatory and market structures between these countries and those of the United States make it difficult to estimate the effects of any similar actions in the United States.

Foreign Jurisdictions Have Taken Actions Regarding Cards

According to information from regulators, card networks, and others, actions regarding card fees, issuer practices, or payment system functioning in general have been taken or considered in as many as 26 countries as well as the European Union in the last 18 years.[39] These actions were described as, among other things, agreements between card networks or issuing banks and governmental authorities, as well as decisions by antitrust tribunals and commissions. For example, in December 2007 the European Commission issued a decision finding that MasterCard's interchange fees for cross-border transactions in the European Economic Area violate European Community Treaty rules on restrictive business practices.[40] In addition, the commission recently announced that it would conduct an inquiry into whether Visa's interchange fees similarly violate the treaty rules.[41] In some cases, the actions taken are under appeal in these jurisdictions.

In reviewing information available from U.S. and foreign regulators, card networks, and other sources, we determined that Australia, Israel, and Mexico had taken actions affecting various parts of their card and payment system markets in recent years, including actions specifically addressing merchant discount or interchange fees. However, data on the impact of the actions taken in these three countries are limited. The following sections summarize the actions in the three countries.

Australia

A 1998 amendment to Australia's Reserve Bank Act created the Payment Systems Board within Australia's central bank, the Reserve Bank of Australia (RBA), and tasks the board with ensuring the efficiency, competition, and stability of that country's payment system. In 2000, RBA published the results of a study that it conducted with the Australian Competition and Consumer Commission, which concluded that prices to cardholders for various forms of card payments did not generally reflect the relative costs of those forms of payments. The authors of the 2000 study noted that merchant discount rates for credit card transactions averaged 1.78 percent, which included average interchange rates of 0.95

[39]Included in the countries identified by the sources are Argentina, Australia, Austria, Brazil, Canada, Chile, Colombia, Denmark, France, Hungary, Israel, Mexico, New Zealand, Norway, Panama, Poland, Portugal, Romania, Singapore, South Africa, South Korea, Spain, Sweden, Switzerland, Turkey, and the United Kingdom. GAO did not conduct an independent survey or in-depth legal analysis of actions taken by foreign countries.

[40]IP/07/1959, Brussels, 19 December 2007.

[41]MEMO/08/170, Brussels, 26 March 2008.

percent. RBA officials explained to us that because card users do not directly pay some of the costs of using cards, including interchange fees, consumers' use of credit cards at the expense of other lower-cost payment methods, such as debit cards was inefficient for their economy as a whole.

To help remedy this perceived inefficiency, RBA first attempted to encourage voluntary action on the part of the credit card industry. When these attempts were unsuccessful, RBA set a ceiling applicable to average credit card interchange rates, which took effect in 2003.[42] RBA officials explained that to determine how to assess appropriate interchange rate levels, they worked with card networks to identify the range of costs incorporated in the calculation of interchange rates. After considering these costs, RBA officials decided that costs associated with transaction processing, fraud and fraud prevention, authorizing transactions, and financing the period between the time the merchant is paid and the time that the issuer receives payment should be covered by the interchange fees, while costs associated with credit losses should not be. To lower interchange rates from their then current levels, the central bank set a benchmark rate that excluded the disallowed costs, and required that the weighted average of the rates set by each four-party credit card system—which at that time included Visa, MasterCard, and a domestic card brand called Bankcard—not exceed that benchmark.[43] RBA officials stated that they chose to use a cost-based method because it appeared to be a transparent and objective way to lower interchange rates. As a result of the reforms, the average interchange rate in the Visa and MasterCard networks declined from 0.95 percent to around 0.50 percent. In addition to the actions taken to limit credit card interchange fees, the central bank also took several other actions designed to promote efficiency and competition in the payment systems during the same period.

Israel

In the late 1990s, officials at the Israel Antitrust Authority (IAA) considered actions to address a lack of competition in their country's credit card market. The market was dominated by two companies, each of which issued and acquired its own major card brand. The rates of merchant discount fees charged by these companies differed according to merchant type, and estimates of the average merchant discount rate at that

---

[42]In Australia, the credit card market is structured differently from the debit card market, and the regulation of debit interchange fees has proceeded in a different manner. We focus our discussion on developments affecting credit card interchange fees.

[43]Bankcard was a domestic credit card that closed in the first half of 2007.

time varied. Some estimated averages reported in 1997 and 1998 ranged from 1.9 percent to 2.46 percent. In 1998, a second company began issuing Visa cards and acquiring Visa transactions in Israel. According to IAA officials, the two Visa issuers executed an agreement between them that included provisions setting the interchange rates applicable to transactions involving their cards. IAA declared the agreement between the companies to be a restraint of trade under Israeli antitrust law, but granted the agreement several exemptions in return for a gradual reduction in the interchange fees, under the condition that Visa conduct an issuer cost study that would provide the IAA with data to establish a suitable and acceptable interchange fee. After these exemptions expired and the IAA found the data provided by the Visa companies to be incomplete, the law required that banks obtain approval of their agreement from the Israeli Antitrust Tribunal—a court with exclusive jurisdiction over noncriminal governmental antitrust proceedings. After years of discussions on the appropriate costs to be covered and different methodologies for setting interchange rates, the Israeli Antitrust Tribunal issued a decision in 2006 that the costs that could be considered in calculating interchange rates included those relating to

- processing transaction authorizations,
- financing the period between when the merchant is paid and when the issuer receives payment, and
- payment guarantee (including both costs involving losses due to cardholder fraud and costs related to prevention of such fraud).

At the same time that this decision was reached, the two Visa issuers, along with Israel's single MasterCard issuer, agreed with IAA to contract with merchants to accept both Visa and MasterCard transactions and to gradually reduce interchange rates. Under this agreement, interchange rates are to gradually drop from their October 2006 level of 1.25 percent to 0.875 percent by 2012. As of January 2007, interchange rates fell to 1.2 percent in keeping with the agreement. In addition, in accordance with the tribunal's decision many of the categories based on merchant type will be eliminated. However, the transactions of government entities that accept cards in Israel will continue to be eligible for a lower interchange rate, also in accordance with the tribunal's decision, under the theory that government entities do not benefit from the payment guarantee, because they have other ways of guaranteeing payment (for example, confiscating assets), and so the interchange fee charged on its acceptance transactions should not include that cost. Although the Antitrust Tribunal has temporarily approved this agreement, it has stated that final approval cannot occur until an independent expert appointed by IAA determines that the agreement is consistent with the tribunal's approved methodology for setting fees.

Mexico

Given responsibility for ensuring the proper functioning of payment systems, the Banco de Mexico (the Mexican central bank) has been encouraging the use of more efficient means of payment. In 2004, the Banco de Mexico was granted specific authority to regulate interchange fees in response to concerns by legislators in that country regarding the amount that banks were charging for services as well as the lack of sufficient information for cardholders and merchants. Shortly after the 2004 law was passed, the Association of Mexican Banks, which establishes interchange rates in Mexico, undertook a review of interchange rates and under the supervision of the Mexican central bank, began to develop a method to set them. In addition, the association and the central bank reviewed the way in which interchange rates applied to merchants. For example, five different interchange rates could be applied to transactions, depending on the merchant's expected annual sales volume, with merchants with higher sales volumes receiving lower rates. Mexican central bank officials explained to us that they believed this led to discrimination against small merchants, and as part of the reforms, the bank association introduced new categories that were based on merchant type rather than size.

To address interchange rates, the bank association under the supervision of Banco de Mexico established a method to set a "reference" interchange rate. In contrast to the cost-based approaches used by Australia and Israel, the bank association used a model that balances issuing and acquiring banks' profits (net of interchange) through the interchange fee. Prior to these developments, the interchange rates for credit cards averaged about 2.73 percent. Since that time rates have declined. In February 2005, the association reduced the credit card interchange rate by an average of 43 basis points and also eliminated the highest bracket of rates for credit cards.[44] Because some of the disadvantages of the previous system persisted despite this intervention, in October 2005 the association proposed a new mechanism for setting a reference interchange rate, which accounts for issuer and acquirer revenues and expected network growth in addition to issuer and acquirer costs. The association then adjusted the

[44] A basis point is equal to .01 percent or 1/100th of a percent.

single reference rate to account for differences in merchant type, resulting in 22 different merchant categories, most of them with different applicable interchange rates. The association and the central bank continue to work together to refine this method. As of January 2008, the effective reference interchange rate for credit cards was lowered to 1.61 percent.

Limited Information on the Effects of Interchange Rate Intervention Suggests Some Benefit to Merchants and a Mixed Picture for Consumers

In the three countries we examined, incomplete information is available on the impact of actions to reduce interchange rates, but available data indicate that merchants appear to have benefited, while the impact on consumers has been mixed. Because the actions relating to interchange rates in these countries generally coincided with various other changes in credit and debit card markets, researchers' ability to isolate and measure the specific effects of interchange rate intervention has been limited. However, merchants in these countries generally appear to have received benefits in the form of lower merchant discount rates. Data on merchant discount rates for credit cards in Australia show a significant decline in these rates since the reforms were instituted and suggest that changes in interchange rates have been reflected in merchant discount rates. The Australian central bank reported that the average merchant discount rate for Bankcard, MasterCard, and Visa had fallen by around 62 basis points to 0.79 percent between the September quarter of 2003, just prior to the reforms, and the December quarter of 2007, which was greater than the decline in interchange rates over that period. Merchant discount rates for American Express and Diners Club cards, although not regulated by the central bank, also fell by 0.29 and 0.18 percentage points, respectively, between September 2003 and December 2007. In September 2007, the central bank estimated that, in the aggregate, merchants' costs for card acceptance over the previous financial year were about $920 million lower than they would have been absent the reforms. Similar reductions also have occurred in Mexico as the credit card merchant discount rates across all businesses declined an average of 8 percent, from 2005 through 2006. According to information provided by IAA, average merchant discount rates have declined in Israel since 1998, especially for Visa cards; however, other factors may have contributed to the overall decline in merchant discount rates in Israel. For example, other regulatory actions relating to limiting merchant discount rates also were being taken during this period. In addition, officials from the antitrust authority expressed the belief that the increased competition in the Visa issuing market since 1998 has contributed to the lower merchant discount rates.

Evidence relating to impacts on consumers since the interchange rate intervention in these countries is limited. In Australia, where the reforms have been in effect long enough to allow for some study, cardholders have experienced a decline in the value of credit card reward points for most cards and an increase in annual and other consumer credit card fees. For example, RBA estimated that average annual fee revenue from fees, such as cash advances and late payments on bank-issued personal credit cards has doubled from around $40 per account in 2002 to around $80 in 2006, although it did not estimate the total amount paid by all cardholders. RBA officials attributed these changes to their reforms of the credit card system. Although card users may receive fewer rewards and experience higher fees when using their cards, consumers in Australia that want to use cards to finance purchases may benefit from the lower-interest cards that issuers began increasingly offering after the reforms were implemented. Regulators indicated that banks altered their business models when interchange fees were reduced to focus more on attracting cardholders who carry a balance. This may have been due, in part, to decreased revenue from interchange fees. In addition, Australia's central bank has not been able to discern whether merchants have passed along their reduction in the costs of accepting cards—resulting from the reforms—in the prices charged for retail goods and services. An RBA official told us, however, that while such an effect would not likely be measurable, he believed competition among merchants would lead merchants to pass some portion of a reduction in their costs along to consumers. RBA's assessment of the reforms' effects on overall welfare is positive and it estimates that welfare gains are likely substantial.

In addition to the impact on merchants and consumers in the three countries we examined, other developments in these countries' payment system markets have occurred since interchange rates were lowered. For example, in Australia, the central bank found that over the past few years, the number and value of debit card payments grew more quickly than those of credit card payments. The central bank stated that this difference reflects slowing growth in the number of credit card transactions—in part resulting from cutbacks in credit card rewards and the introduction of surcharges—as well as increasing growth in the number of debit card transactions due in part to new types of deposit accounts offered by banks that make debit card transactions more attractive. Additionally, the combined market share of MasterCard, Visa, and Bankcard decreased, and the combined market share of American Express and Diners Club correspondingly increased by about 1 percent to around 16 percent of the value of credit card transactions.[45] The Mexican central bank reports that the number of credit and debit card payments increased significantly in the last few years. In addition, several new banks have entered the issuing and acquiring markets and concentration in these markets has decreased, although both markets still continue to be relatively concentrated compared to that of the United States. In Israel, IAA officials told us that too little time has passed to evaluate the effects of their reforms; however, they expect that the creation of a single interchange system will yield efficiency gains and promote competition for the benefit of consumers.

Potential Effects of Taking Similar Actions on Interchange Fees in the United States Are Uncertain

The extent to which similar actions to lower interchange rates in the United States might reduce costs to merchants and consumers is unclear. While actions in the three countries examined appear to have reduced the costs to merchants for accepting cards, less information was available on the impact on consumers. In Australia, for example, costs for card users appear to have increased, but having these individuals experience higher costs could be considered more efficient and appropriate than merchants passing their card acceptance costs along to all consumers through higher prices for goods and services, as RBA concluded was occurring before the reforms. However, whether consumers choosing to make purchases with other forms of payment have experienced any benefits was not clear.

In addition, variations in payment systems across the countries we studied suggest that interchange levels may not be the only relevant factor to consider when examining card costs in the United States compared with those of other countries. For example, although average interchange rates for credit cards in the United States are higher than the rates that have been set in the countries we reviewed, one industry group found in 2005 that the amount of the processing fee component included in the total merchant discount rate applied to credit card acceptance transactions in many other developed countries around the world is actually greater than in the United States. Therefore, comparing only interchange rates may not give an accurate picture of the relative costs of card acceptance to merchants. Further, because interchange rates are reportedly intended to balance costs across consumers, merchants, and issuing and acquiring banks, differences in interchange levels between the United States and other countries could be the result of different cost structures for the

[45]In Australia, until recently American Express cards were issued exclusively by American Express in a proprietary model similar to that in the United States.

banks in these markets. For example, Israel has fewer than 10 card issuers, and officials at the Federal Reserve Bank of Kansas City estimated in 2006 that the four largest banks in Australia issued 55 percent of cards. In contrast, we reported in 2006 that the United States has more than 6,000 depository institutions that issue credit cards, and therefore the costs of issuing credit cards in this country could be different than in countries with many fewer issuing banks.[46]

Finally, the regulatory and legal structure in the United States differs from those of other countries. For example, unlike in Australia and other countries we reviewed, in the United States there is no entity specifically tasked with regulating or overseeing the competitive aspects of the interchange fee structure or the fees' effects on consumers. To the extent that the imposition of interchange fees would constitute an anticompetitive or unfair business practice prohibited by the antitrust laws or the Federal Trade Commission Act, the Department of Justice (DOJ) and FTC, respectively, could take measures to ensure compliance with those laws. In 1998, DOJ sued Visa and MasterCard for alleged antitrust violations relating to the networks' "exclusivity rules," which prohibited member banks from issuing Discover or American Express cards.[47] The court found that the exclusivity rules were a substantial restraint on competition in violation of the Sherman Act. Although the imposition of interchange fees was not found to violate the law, the trial court noted that the defendants' ability to impose and change the fees was evidence of market power, which was an element in proving the anticompetitive nature of the exclusivity rules.[48] Further, DOJ officials told us that under its authority to enforce the antitrust laws, DOJ is again looking into issues concerning the payment systems industry. (Also, as previously noted, interchange fees have been a factor in lawsuits alleging violations of the federal antitrust laws by credit card networks and related parties. In addition, private parties are pursuing civil actions that address interchange fees under these same laws.[49]) FTC officials expressed to us the view that the FTC does not have authority to regulate interchange fees. Also,

---

[46]GAO-06-929, p.10.

[47]*United States v. Visa U.S.A., Inc.*, 163 F. Supp. 2d 322 (S.D.N.Y. 2001), *aff'd*, 344 F.3d 229 (2d Cir 2003), *Cert. Denied*, 543 U.S. 811 (2004).

[48]163 F. Supp. 2d at 340; see 244 F. 3d at 239-40.

[49]In re Payment Card Interchange Fee and Merchant Discount Antitrust Litigation, 398 F. Supp.2d 1356 (E.D. NY Oct. 19, 2005).

officials of the Board of Governors of the Federal Reserve noted that the Federal Reserve does not have a specific mandate to regulate interchange fees in the United States.[50]

Card Usage by Federal Entities Provides Numerous Benefits, but Creates Control Challenges

Many federal entities use cards to make purchases of goods and services needed for their operations, spending more than $27 billion on purchase, travel, and fleet cards in fiscal year 2007.[51] Officials we interviewed from five federal entities that were high-volume users of cards for goods, travel, and automotive expenses told us that using cards reduces their administrative expenses, provides income from the rebates they receive from the issuing banks, and provides other benefits. Although generally citing few drawbacks to the use of charge cards, federal entity officials acknowledged challenges in controlling use of cards, but also noted that the data available on card use and tools provided by the issuing banks help them address these challenges.

Entities' Use of Cards Has Grown Significantly and Is Expected to Increase Further

More than 350 federal entities participate in GSA's SmartPay program—which provides purchase, travel, and fleet cards for these entities to use. Federal entities pay no direct costs for the general use of cards.[52] According to card network officials, the banks that issue cards to federal entities are compensated in part by the interchange fees they receive when a government entity or employee uses a card to make a purchase.

In fiscal year 2007, federal entities used cards to purchase more than $27 billion of goods and services. This represents an inflation-adjusted increase of 51 percent over fiscal year 1999 spending levels (see fig. 2). Most of this spending occurred using purchase cards, which account for nearly 70 percent of total federal entity card spending, while about one-quarter of card spending was done using travel cards and about 5 percent using fleet cards. The number of transactions has also increased by 50 percent since 1999, from about 60 million transactions to over 90 million in

[50]The Board of Governors of the Federal Reserve has regulatory authority over the processing of payments but does not regulate the fees that banks pay for participating in private credit card payments systems.

[51]Fleet cards are used for fuel and supplies for government vehicles.

[52]Although federal entities pay no direct costs to issuing banks for the general use of cards, some products and services, such as traveler's checks, do entail fees.

2007. However, the rate of growth of both spending and transactions has slowed in recent years.

Figure 2: SmartPay Spending and Total Number of Transactions, Fiscal Years 1999-2007

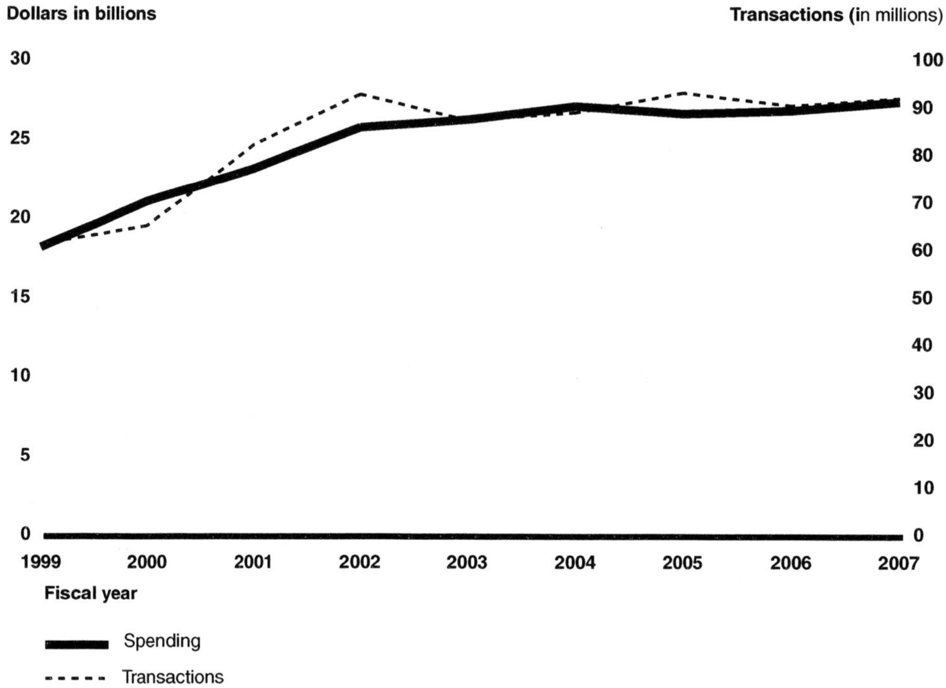

Source: GAO analysis of GSA data.

Note: Spending amounts adjusted for inflation to constant 2007 dollars.

According to the Director of GSA's Office of Charge Card Management, the increases in spending and the number of transactions in the early years of the SmartPay program were due to entities adjusting their purchasing behaviors from previously used systems, such as purchase orders, and learning how to use their cards to make additional purchases. Although the number of transactions remained roughly constant between fiscal years 2002 and 2007, the average transaction value rose from about $240 to about $300, accounting for the growth in total spending during this time. According to the Director, the number of transactions has remained relatively stable in current years because, for the most part, entities have transitioned from most of their previously used purchasing systems and are now making only small changes to their programs to improve efficiencies.

The Director of GSA's Office of Charge Card Management also told us that card use by federal entities is expected to continue growing as the entities identify additional ways of using cards and implement new payment technologies. For example, officials from the Department of Veterans Affairs (VA) told us that they are working with the bank that issues the department's purchase cards to find new ways to increase card usage. They explained that in 2003 they developed a process for making payments through the card system to non-VA medical providers for services provided to veterans who are unable to visit a VA center for medical care, reducing the number of checks they must issue and increasing both the number of electronic payments made and their card use rebates. Additionally, officials stated that VA is reviewing its purchase records to attempt to shift more purchasing to vendors that accept cards. Similarly, the U.S. Army has developed an automated payment system that uses purchase cards for most of the $400 million per year it pays schools and other institutions for soldiers' tuition assistance. GSA officials also expect the new products and services that will be available under the SmartPay 2 program will lead to increases in overall card spending. Some of these products include prepaid cards, contactless cards, and cards in foreign currencies.[53]

Officials Cite Various Benefits Associated with Using Cards, Including Administrative Cost Savings and Rebates

According to federal entity officials we spoke with, one of the primary benefits associated with card usage is the administrative cost savings compared with procurement methods that card usage has partially replaced, such as purchase orders, imprest funds, and blanket purchase agreements. For example, obtaining goods or services under a purchase order system requires that a purchase request be filled out and approved, then sent to a procurement office, which issues it to a vendor. When government entities use a card, however, goods or services can be directly purchased by cardholders, who then review their statements at the end of the billing cycle and forward the statement to an approving official. Officials from the Department of Agriculture said that if cards were not used, staff would need to complete purchase orders for each of the 1.5 million transactions per year that currently are made using purchase cards. Officials from the Department of Homeland Security estimated that the department would require four to five times the current number of

[53] A prepaid card is one that is programmed to have a monetary value, and charges to that card cannot exceed the balance. Contactless cards store data on a microchip embedded in the card, which can be read by passing the card in front of a special card reader.

staff who operate its travel card program if it paid for travel expenses without cards. In addition, officials at the Department of Agriculture stated that new tools, such as an automated process to reset charge card passwords, may further reduce the costs of administering their program.

Estimates of per transaction administrative costs savings from card usage vary, making it difficult to estimate total administrative cost savings. GSA estimated total administrative cost savings from card use in fiscal year 2006 to be $1.7 billion. An official from GSA told us that this estimate was based on per transaction saving estimates by the Purchase Card Council. In 1994, the council, an interagency group, asked 17 civilian government organizations to perform a detailed cost-benefit analysis comparing the use of purchase orders versus purchase cards for transactions of $2,500 and below. The per transaction savings estimates for the 17 organizations ranged from $1.42 to more than $142, with an average of about $54. More recently, in a 2006 research study, the Association of Government Accountants surveyed four civilian agencies with an approach similar to that of the Purchase Card Council and reported savings estimates of $60 to $166 per transaction, with a weighted average of about $87.[54] In comparison, a 2005 survey of almost 1,300 purchase card program administrators from corporations, nonprofits, and government entities found, for state and federal government entities, a $53 administrative cost savings per transaction compared to purchase orders.[55] Finally, a 1997 analysis by the U.S. Army Audit Agency showed that the average cost to the U.S. Army of processing a purchase order was about $155 compared to about $62 for a card, a savings of about $93 per transaction.[56]

Another benefit of card use for federal entities is the receipt of rebates from the banks that issue their cards. Rebate amounts, which, after adjusting for inflation, have almost doubled since fiscal year 2002 to $175 million in fiscal year 2007 (see fig. 3), are based on a number of factors, mainly the volume of net spending on cards and how quickly balances on the cards are paid. GSA establishes a minimum rebate rate that federal entities should receive, but entities can choose to negotiate with their

[54]AGA Corporate Partner Advisory Group Research, "The Federal Purchase Card: Use, Policy, and Best Practice," *AGA CPAG Research Series*, Report No. 4 (April 2006).

[55]Richard J. Palmer and Mahendra Gupta, "The 2005 Purchasing Card Benchmark Survey Report" (2006).

[56]U.S. Army Audit Agency, "Savings from Acquisition Reform" Audit Report: AA 97-58 (Alexandria, Virginia: Jan. 7, 1997).

issuing banks for additional amounts. Between 1998 and 2007, the minimum rate was 6 basis points of the net volume of spending on the cards, while under the SmartPay 2 program, the minimum rebate rate will increase to 8 basis points.[57] A GSA official stated that typically in federal entities' negotiations with issuing banks, the rebate rate is increased as an incentive for an entity to choose a particular bank to issue its cards. According to the GSA official, however, some entities negotiate for specialized services rather than increased rebate amounts, and GSA encourages agencies to examine their programs holistically when negotiating terms.

Figure 3: Total Rebates Received from SmartPay Card Use, Fiscal Years 2002-2007

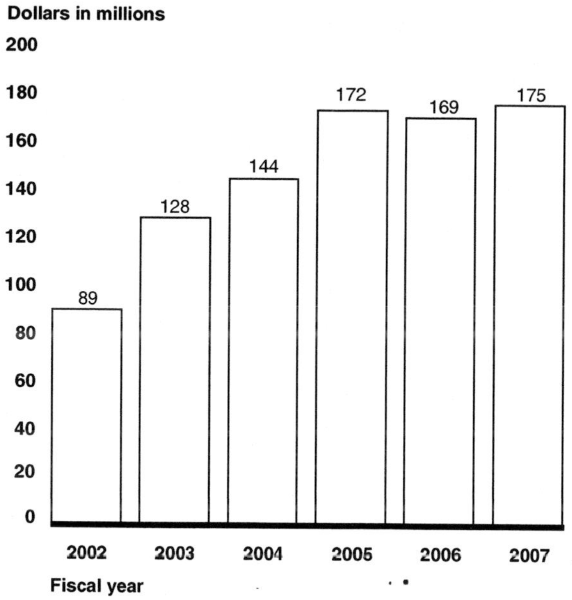

Source: GAO analysis of GSA data.

Note: Rebate amounts adjusted for inflation to 2007 constant dollars.

Federal entities differ in how they use their rebates. Two of the federal entities we spoke with return the rebates directly to the location that originated the relevant transaction, one adds the rebates into general

[57]GSA receives 4 of the basis points, termed the Industrial Funding Fee. This fee totaled approximately $9 million in fiscal year 2007 and is used by GSA to administer the SmartPay program as well as one other GSA program.

income for the entity, and one other allocates rebates to a working capital fund for initiatives of general benefit to the entity.

Officials from federal entities also cited several other benefits associated with using cards to make purchases. For example, officials from several entities told us that the increased data on purchases that is available to them by using charge cards allows for better management and/or tracking of spending. According to officials at the Department of Agriculture, purchase card data allowed them to examine their purchasing patterns and identify opportunities for savings. They explained that by using purchase cards to buy office supplies, they received data on the transactions, which they used to negotiate a contract with a vendor to buy supplies in bulk that resulted in millions of dollars in savings per year.[58] Officials from several entities also told us that cards allow them to make purchases more quickly and/or more conveniently than previously used methods of purchasing. For example, officials from one entity told us that once the approval process is completed for a particular purchase, it can be made immediately, whereas previously used methods take a longer time to complete. According to officials from another entity, the ability to obtain cash advances on cards benefits them because it eliminates the need for imprest funds, which, according to officials from a different entity, are harder to monitor for fraud. Other benefits cited by officials from one entity included compensating vendors doing business with the government more quickly and greater ability to resolve disputes with vendors because charges can be reversed until the dispute is resolved.

While Minimizing Card Abuse Poses Control Challenges, Banks Provide Tools to Help Entities Address Them

Officials at the federal entities with whom we met cited only a few drawbacks associated with the use of cards, though officials from some entities mentioned the risk of fraud and misuse. However, these officials told us that the risk of these occurrences is less than or equal to that under previously used procurement systems. Although the instances of fraud and misuse on cards may be infrequent, we and several inspectors general have reported internal control weaknesses in charge card programs at federal entities and instances of fraud and abuse. For example, in 2001 and 2002 we issued reports on control weaknesses in purchase card programs

[58]We have previously reported that the use of purchase cards presents an opportunity for entities to negotiate discounts from major purchase card vendors, but agencies generally have not seized those opportunities. See GAO, *Contract Management: Agencies Can Achieve Significant Savings on Purchase Card Buys*, GAO-04-430 (Washington, D.C.: Mar. 12, 2004).

at the Air Force, Army, and Navy. The reports contained over 100 recommendations targeted at improving the design and implementation of controls over card use and establishing guidelines for disciplining those who misuse their government purchase cards.[59] In 2003, we reported that the military services had begun or implemented nearly all of those recommendations, some of which were included in legislative requirements for the Department of Defense.[60] In addition, earlier this year we reported on breakdowns in internal controls in various federal entity purchase card programs, which in some instances resulted in fraudulent, improper, and abusive use of purchase cards.[61]

For the most part, fraud and misuse can be limited through strong internal controls in card programs of federal entities. GSA and OMB have issued guidance on internal controls intended to reduce the risk of misuse of cards. For example, GSA develops guidance through training courses for federal entities and publishes guidelines for oversight and information on detecting misuse and fraud. Additionally, OMB has issued several memorandums related to oversight of card programs. For example, a 2002 OMB memorandum provided that each federal entity review the adequacy of its internal controls for purchase and travel card expenditures, and required entities to submit action plans detailing any risks associated with these programs and identifying the internal controls that will be used to manage these risks. In 2005, OMB also issued an appendix to its 1995 circular on management accountability and control, which consolidated and updated governmentwide card program requirements and included minimum requirements and best practices on several aspects of card programs. Some of the best practices to limit fraud and misuse identified in these guidance documents included implementing appropriate training for cardholders, approving officials, and other staff; deactivating cards that

[59]GAO, *Purchase Cards: Control Weaknesses Leave Two Navy Units Vulnerable to Fraud and Abuse*, GAO-02-32 (Washington D.C.: Nov. 30, 2001); *Purchase Cards: Control Weaknesses Leave Army Vulnerable to Fraud, Waste, and Abuse*, GAO-02-732 (Washington, D.C.: June 27, 2002); *Purchase Cards: Navy Is Vulnerable to Fraud and Abuse but Is Taking Action to Resolve Control Weaknesses*, GAO-02-1041 (Washington D.C.: Sept. 27, 2002); *Purchase Cards: Control Weaknesses Leave the Air Force Vulnerable to Fraud, Waste, and Abuse*, GAO-03-292 (Washington, D.C.: Dec. 20, 2002).

[60]GAO, *Purchase Cards: Steps Taken to Improve DOD Program Management but Actions Needed to Address Misuse*, GAO-04-156 (Washington, D.C.: Dec. 2, 2003).

[61]GAO, *Governmentwide Purchase Cards: Actions Needed to Strengthen Internal Controls to Reduce Fraudulent, Improper, and Abusive Purchases*, GAO-08-333 (Washington D.C.: Mar. 14, 2008).

are not used; requiring charge card transaction or statement reconciliation on the part of the cardholder in a timely manner; ensuring managerial review of charge card purchases; and implementing policies outlining appropriate administrative and/or disciplinary actions for charge card misuse.

Finally, officials from some of the federal entities we interviewed told us that the tools and data provided by their card-issuing banks helped them to limit the risk of misuse of cards by enabling them to track and limit the types of purchases made on the cards. For example, some entities block the use of cards at certain merchant types, to help ensure that the cards are used only for approved goods and services, or limit transaction amounts, cash withdrawals, and other activities. Officials from several entities noted that the data on card transactions they receive from their issuing bank allow them to monitor for potentially fraudulent or inappropriate transactions. For example, an official from one entity told us that the data allowed it to identify suspicious transactions based on specified dollar amounts, charges to certain vendors, and other types of transactions that could involve misuse. Officials from another entity noted that security features on cards help identify suspect charges by generating alerts for questionable transactions and by sending an e-mail to the cardholder every time a transaction occurs on his or her account in order to verify whether the transaction was approved by the cardholder.

Conclusions

Federal entities' acceptance of credit and debit cards provides a number of benefits, including client and customer convenience, but also entails costs. In collecting over $27 billion in revenue via cards in 2007, the transactions of federal entities included within the scope of this report resulted in more than $430 million in merchant discount fees, including at least $205 million in interchange fees (paid by entities that provided us with data specifically on interchange fees). Federal entities have undertaken a number of worthwhile actions to ensure that card acceptance costs are minimized. Further, FMS's program to comprehensively examine the revenue sources and collection mechanisms used by the many entities for which it performs collections shows great promise for achieving savings and identifying improvements for revenue collection, whether through cards or other mechanisms. Since its initiation on a pilot basis in 2007, this program has already identified potential cost savings or efficiency improvements at the eight entities FMS has examined to date. Because such savings would be recurring—in that they are applicable to future transactions—this program appears to be a valuable effort for FMS to complete in a timely manner. Ensuring that FMS's program implementation strategy has additional elements, such as a timeline for completing the reviews, cost savings estimates, and an assessment of the adequacy of the resources committed will increase the likelihood of FMS achieving its goals as expeditiously as possible. Establishing a timeline for completion would allow FMS management to determine whether the program is being implemented expeditiously, including taking action if interim milestones are not being met. Generating cost savings estimates would appear to provide FMS with an additional tool for prompting entities to implement the improvements that are identified. Further, establishing a timeline for monitoring progress and estimating the cost savings to be realized could also allow FMS to better assess whether the level of resources committed to the program is appropriate. Perhaps most important, developing a full implementation strategy would allow FMS to identify potential cost savings for its collection activities—and federal entities to begin realizing them—more quickly, resulting in larger overall financial benefits to the government.

Other countries have examined the significance of interchange fees as part of credit and debit card payments, and several have taken or are considering actions to improve efficiencies and reduce costs involving their card payment systems. In one of the three countries we examined that has acted to limit interchange fees, available evidence suggests that the costs for merchants from accepting cards has declined but the direct costs for consumers using cards may have increased. However, a number of factors may be influencing costs, and additional data and study would be needed to more definitively assess the effects of these actions. Further adding to the difficulty of estimating the potential effects of such actions in the United States, are differences in the structure and regulation of the U.S. card payment market from those of the other countries we examined.

Federal entities have realized benefits from using cards to make purchases of needed goods and services, including supplies, travel expenses, and vehicle operating costs, and have taken actions to address the challenge of ensuring that cards are used only for intended purposes. In addition to increased efficiency in administrative processes and cost savings, in fiscal year 2007 card use also produced about $175 million in additional operating funds through the rebates provided by the banks that issue government cards. Agencies have acknowledged the continuing need to ensure adequate monitoring and to have controls in place to minimize fraudulent and abusive use of their cards. The ability to analyze data on card activities—a capability that the issuing banks are providing to agencies—appears to be a valuable tool, in that it helps federal entities manage their card activities and potentially reduces costs for the government.

APPENDIX I: OBJECTIVES, SCOPE AND METHODOLOGY

Our objectives were to examine (1) the benefits and costs, including interchange fees, associated with federal entities' acceptance of cards as payment for the sale of goods, services, and revenue collection; (2) actions taken in countries that have regulated or otherwise limited interchange fees and their impact; and (3) the impact on federal entities of using cards to make purchases.

To determine the benefits received by federal entities from the acceptance of credit and debit cards, we conducted semistructured interviews with five judgmentally selected federal entities that participate in Financial Management Service's (FMS) Credit and Debit Card Acquiring Service, which is a governmentwide service that allows federal entities to accept payment by Visa, MasterCard, American Express, and Discover cards, as well as some types of debit cards. FMS provides this service to any executive, judicial, and legislative branch agency; government corporation; commission; board; or other federal entity that determines that the acceptance of cards is needed for revenue collection. Three of the five entities we contacted were among those that conducted the highest volume of card transactions, and two entities were among those that conducted the lowest volume of card transactions.[1] We also reviewed and summarized studies and reports on the costs associated with processing different forms of payment to identify how these costs compared with the costs associated with card acceptance.

To estimate the costs associated with federal entities' acceptance of cards as payment, we collected data from as broad a range of entities associated with the federal government as possible. To determine the federal entities from which to collect data, we met with FMS who provided us with data on all federal entities that participate in its Credit and Debit Card Acquiring Service. FMS provided us data on revenues collected through card transactions and the merchant discount, interchange, and processing fees it paid for these entities' acceptance of cards for fiscal years 2005 through 2007. Additionally, FMS officials provided us with a list of Department of Defense and Department of Homeland Security nonappropriated fund instrumentalities that have independent authority to collect revenue and thus handle their own card collections. We reviewed data for these entities as well. These entities included

[1]The federal entities that had high volumes of card acceptance were the Defense Commissary Agency, U.S. Mint, and the Department of the Interior's National Park Service. The federal entities that had low volumes of card acceptance were the Corporation for National and Community Service and the National Endowment for the Arts.

- Air Force Services Agency,
- U.S. Army and MWR Command,
- Army and Air Force Exchange Service,
- Marine Corps Community Services,
- Navy Exchange Service Command,
- Navy Morale, Welfare and Recreation,
- Coast Guard Exchange System, and
- Coast Guard Morale, Well-being, and Recreation.

The U.S. Postal Service, Amtrak, and Smithsonian Institution operate their own card collection programs as well and do not utilize FMS's services, thus we collected data directly from those entities for fiscal years 2005 through 2007. Smithsonian Institution and the Coast Guard Morale, Well-being, and Recreation were unable to provide us data on their card collection programs for this period of time because they do not maintain centralized program data on card revenues and fees. Instead, their card operations are decentralized among the various locations in which they operate. We also collected data from two private entities that accept tax payments made by credit and debit cards on behalf of the Internal Revenue Service (IRS). These two entities—Official Payments Corporation and LINK2GOV—provide this service at no cost to IRS and instead charge taxpayers who choose to use their services a convenience fee for doing so. While we report the card acceptance fees associated with federal tax payments for these two entities, we do not include them in the total amount of card acceptance fees paid by federal entities. We did not attempt to determine additional federal entities beyond those listed here that may operate their own card collection programs and therefore pay fees related to card acceptance.

From each of the entities that we collected data, we requested three pieces of information for fiscal years 2005 through 2007:

- total amount of revenue collected in credit and debit cards,
- total amount of interchange fees assessed on card transactions, and

- total amount of merchant discount fees (for processing fees as well as interchange fees) assessed on card transactions.

Only three entities—Amtrak, FMS, and the Postal Service—were able to separately identify the amounts they paid in interchange fees. For the other entities, we obtained the total amounts paid in merchant discount fees. The data we collected on the costs associated with card acceptance from the federal entities were the best data available; however, because of limitations in and differences among the record keeping of the entities, the data may not be complete for all years, may treat some costs inconsistently, and in one case contain estimated, rather than actual, values. For example, not all entities could provide us with complete data for all 3 fiscal years, and some entities treated certain costs inconsistently, such as including cost information for chargeback fees in their merchant discount fee data.[2] In another case, a federal entity used data from other time periods to estimate some of the pieces of information we requested. We reviewed these data for completeness and accuracy and determined that none of the limitations materially affect the findings we report. However, due to these limitations, the actual figures presented are best viewed as approximations, or estimates in some cases, rather than precise figures. The dollar values for this objective are reported as current dollars.

In addition to analyzing data from federal entities on the revenues and costs associated with card acceptance, we also reviewed some federal entities' contracts or agreements with acquiring banks. To determine the interchange fees applicable to the federal entities' card transactions, as well as the factors that cause interchange fees to vary, we reviewed MasterCard and Visa interchange rate schedules effective beginning October 2007 and April 2008. We also reviewed historical interchange rate schedules for rates that were effective August 2003 through April 2007 that were provided by an acquiring bank. Additionally, we interviewed government officials responsible for settling card transactions, and officials from American Express Company, Discover Financial Services, MasterCard Incorporated, Visa Inc., and Fifth Third Bancorp—FMS's current acquiring bank—to gather information on how government entities' card acceptance fees are assessed and steps being taken to manage the fees.

---

[2]A chargeback fee is any disputed credit or signature debit sale that is returned to an acquiring entity for reimbursement of the cardholder's account.

To examine actions taken in countries that have limited interchange fees, we reviewed available literature, contacted our counterparts (other audit institutions) in several countries, and interviewed Federal Reserve and industry officials to identify various countries where regulators or others had taken such actions. We judgmentally selected countries for further examination from among those identified based on three criteria: (1) actions had been taken that required actually determining interchange rates, (2) information available on the methods they used to determine the rates had been made available (3) efforts had been under way for sufficient time to allow for study. To allow for illustration of diverse approaches to limiting interchange fees, we sought to include countries that had taken different types of actions. In addition, in order to study the impacts of these actions, we sought to include countries where the effects of the intervention had been the subject of empirical study. On the basis of these criteria, we selected three countries—Australia, Israel, and Mexico—for more detailed study. We conducted further literature reviews on these countries and conducted interviews with officials involved in the efforts to limit rates in each of these countries to learn about the measures taken, other measures that were considered, and any empirical data on the effects of the interchange limitation. Additionally, we met with officials from the Board of Governors of the Federal Reserve System, Department of Justice, and the Federal Trade Commission to learn how the regulatory and legal structure in the United States addresses interchange fees.

To determine the impact on federal entities of using cards to make purchases, we obtained and analyzed fiscal years 1999 through 2007 General Services Administration (GSA) SmartPay program data on spending, transactions, and rebates received. On the basis of our review and testing of GSA's data for a separate engagement, we determined that these data were sufficiently reliable for the purposes of this engagement. Dollar values have been adjusted for this objective to fiscal year 2007 constant dollars using the gross domestic product (GDP) price index.[3] Additionally, we reviewed policies and procedures related to card usage from GSA and other government entities, as well as our prior reports, and academic and government reports. To obtain their views on the benefits and drawbacks of card usage, we interviewed officials from GSA, 5 federal entities that were among the 10 entities with the highest spending and most transactions on cards in fiscal year 2006, the bank that issued cards

[3]Based on U.S. Department of Commerce, Bureau of Economic Analysis, National Income and Product Accounts, table 1.1.4, last revised Jan 30, 2008.

which accounted for the highest government card spending in fiscal year 2006, and one academic researcher with extensive work on government use of cards.

We conducted this performance audit from June 2007 to May 2008 in accordance with generally accepted government auditing standards. Those standards require that we plan and perform the audit to obtain sufficient, appropriate evidence to provide a reasonable basis for our findings and conclusions based on our audit objectives. We believe that the evidence obtained provides a reasonable basis for our findings and conclusions based on our audit objectives.

Appendix II: Summary of Major Federal Antitrust Actions Surrounding Interchange Rates

The following identifies key cases concerning interchange fees.

NaBanco

In this 1980s case, NaBanco claimed that the setting of credit card interchange fees by Visa member banks constituted unlawful price fixing.[1] NaBanco was a third-party enterprise that processed credit card transactions for its client acquiring banks, who were members of the Visa network. NaBanco alleged that the imposition of an interchange fee affected the amount it could collect for its service, and that under Visa's rules the fee had an anticompetitive effect. The court ruled that NaBanco did not satisfy its burden of proof under a "rule of reason" analysis to show that interchange fees were a restraint of trade.

Department of Justice proceeding

In 1998, Department of Justice (DOJ) sued Visa and MasterCard for alleged antitrust violations.[2] In that proceeding, the government focused on two points. First, the department claimed that because the boards of Visa and MasterCard were dominated by many of the same banks, intersystem competition was reduced. Second, DOJ challenged the networks' "exclusivity rules," which prohibited member banks from issuing Discover or American Express cards. The court ruled against the government on the first claim (DOJ did not appeal) but found that the exclusivity rules were a substantial restraint on competition in violation of the Sherman Act. The district court invalidated the exclusivity rules, enjoined the defendants from restricting banks from issuing other cards, and permitted Visa and MasterCard issuers to terminate any contractual obligations to abide by the exclusivity rules. Although the imposition of interchange fees was not found to violate the law, the court noted that the defendants' ability to impose and change the fees was evidence of market power, which was an element in proving the anticompetitive nature of the exclusivity rules.[3]

---

[1]*National Bancard Corp. v. Visa U.S.A., Inc.* 596 F. Supp. 1231 (S.D. Fla 1984), *aff'd.* 779 F.2d 592 (11th Cir. 1986).

[2]*United States v. Visa U.S.A., Inc.*, 163 F . Supp. 2d . 322 (S.D.N.Y. 2001), *aff'd*, 344 F.3d 229 (2d Cir 2003), *Cert. Denied*, 543 U.S. 811 (2004).

[3]163 F. Supp. 2d at 340; see 244 F. 3d at 239-40.

Pending Class Action—U. S. District Court (E.D.N.Y.)

In a class action pending in the United States District Court for the Eastern District of New York, merchants claim that interchange fees have an anticompetitive effect in violation of the federal antitrust laws. This case is a consolidation of numerous separate actions. As of October 2005, merchants had instituted 14 class action lawsuits in four separate districts against Visa and MasterCard and their member banks. According to the Magistrate Judge assigned to the consolidated case, as of February 2006 "some forty class action lawsuits" had been brought "on behalf of a class of merchants against the defendant credit card networks and certain of their member banks."[5]

Kendall decision

In March 2008, the Federal Court of Appeals for the Ninth Circuit upheld the District Court's dismissal of a claim in which merchants alleged that the merchant discount fees set by Visa, MasterCard, Bank of America, Wells Fargo Bank, and U.S. Bank violated Section 1 of the Sherman Act,15 U.S.C. § 1, and Section 16 of the Clayton Act, 15 U.S.C. § 26.[6] The court ruled that the plaintiffs failed to plead evidentiary facts necessary to support such a claim. Specifically, the court found that the merchants failed to allege facts necessary to support their theory that the banks conspired or agreed with each other or with Visa and MasterCard to restrain trade. With respect to the allegations against the banks, the court observed that "merely charging, adopting or following the fees set by a Consortium is insufficient as a matter of law to constitute a violation of Section 1 of the Sherman Act." Further, the court concluded that the interchange fee set by Visa and MasterCard was not imposed directly upon the merchants as an anticompetitive measure but instead constituted a cost imposed on the banks which the banks passed on to the merchants as a rational business decision.

---

[4]In re Payment Card Interchange Fee and Merchant Discount Antitrust Litigation, 398 F. Supp.2d 1356 (E.D. NY Oct. 19, 2005).

[5]In re Payment Card Interchange Fee and Merchant Discount Antitrust Litigation, 2006 U.S. Dist. LEXIS 45727; 2006-1 Trade Cas. (CCH) P75,278 (E.D.N.Y.)

[6]*Kendall v. Visa U.S.A., Inc.*, 518 F.3d 1042 (9th Cir. 2008).

Index

A

B

C

D

E

F

G

H

I

J

L

M

N

U

V

W

Y